The Little Book
of
WIT &
WISDOM

The Little Book
of
WIT &

WISDOM

Edited by

ROSANNA KELLY *and*

ELIZA PAKENHAM

mustard

First published in 1999 by Mustard
Mustard is an imprint of Parragon

Parragon
Queen Street House
4 Queen Street
Bath BA1 1HE UK

Produced by Magpie Books, an imprint of
Robinson Publishing Ltd, London

ISBN 1 84164 265 7

A copy of the British Library Cataloguing-in-Publication Data
is available from the British Library

Contents

To our grandparents

Introduction

"Wisdom," said the Duc de la Rochefoucauld, "is to the soul what health is to the body"; whilst Alexander Pope once defined wit as "what oft was thought but ne'er so well expressed." Best of all in combination, here then are some sparks of wit and wisdom through the ages, to advise, console and amuse the reader.

The first section, The Art of Living has practical advice on money, work, career, even on playing bridge, and some hints on how to approach everyday life. Montaigne, for example, recommended "continual cheerfulness" as "the most certain sign of wisdom." In contrast, in Thoughts on Politics, witty rhetoric marks out the great and good, and the not so good, in the field of government. Here you'll find Abraham Lincoln's famous comment on the nature of leadership: "You can fool all the people some of the time, and some of the people all the time, but you cannot fool all the people all the time," or Winston Churchill's definition of political ability ". . . to foretell what is going to happen tomorrow, next week, next month and next year. And to have the ability afterward to explain why it didn't happen."

The section on Society and Friendship affirms that friendship is one of the best things that life has to offer, but that it is not always serene. There are wise thoughts on how to succeed on the social stage without making enemies, and how to tell a good friend from a bad. Widely commented on in the next section are the age-old themes of Love and Marriage. Long ago Ovid declared "From high above, Jupiter laughs at those who love," so there is plenty of advice to lovers from both the sexes — anyone reading it carefully may think twice about tying the knot. (Especially if Iris Murdoch was right when she observed "Every man needs two women, a quiet homemaker and a thrilling nymph.") Youth and Age leaps nervously into the generation gap, and concludes with relief that although older is by no means wiser, as Jerry Garcia says: ". . . if you stick around long enough, you eventually get respectable." In Time Flies, we are reminded that time is a theme with which many great philosophers have grappled, including Groucho Marx who put it succinctly: "Time wounds all heels," though some may not agree with him. And before time flies away with us entirely, we come to some Final Reflections, perfect for pondering in the spare moments of our busy lives. As it goes in Punch: "Sometimes I sits and thinks, and then again I just sits."

For all their excellent help in helping us find witty and wise quotations, we'd like to thank a good many friends and relations, but particularly Linda Kelly and Alex Chisholm.

Chapter 1

THE ART OF LIVING

I always pass on good advice. It is the only thing to do with it. It is never of any use to oneself.
Oscar Wilde, *The Picture of Dorian Gray*

The art of living is more like wrestling than dancing, in as much as it, too, demands a firm and watchful stance against any unexpected onset.
Marcus Aurelius, *Meditations*

Some witty and cheering advice on how best to wrestle with life.

Quiet calm deliberation disentangles every knot.

W.S. Gilbert, *The Mikado*

Noble deeds and hot baths are the best cure for depression.

Dodie Smith, *I Capture the Castle*.

Curtsey while you're thinking what to say. It saves time.

Lewis Carroll, *Through the Looking-Glass*

Never complain and never explain.

Benjamin Disraeli, in J. Morley's *Life of Gladstone*

Never give in, never give in, never, never, never, never – in nothing, great or small, large or petty – never give in except to convictions of honour and good sense.

Winston Churchill, speech at Harrow school, 29 Oct. 1941

Man is only truly great when he acts from the passions.

Benjamin Disraeli, *Coningsby*

The heights of great men reached and kept
Were not achieved by sudden flight,
But they, while their companions slept
Were toiling upward in the night.

Henry Wadsworth Longfellow, from
"The Ladder of St Augustine"

Genius does what it must, and Talent does what it can.

> Edward Robert Bulwer, Earl of Lytton,
> *Last Words of a Sensitive Second-Rate Poet*

For, those that fly, may fight again,
Which he can never do that's slain.

> Samuel Butler, from *"Hudibras"*

More haste, less speed.

> English proverb

Lord, temper with tranquillity,
Our manifold activity,
That we may do our work for Thee,
With very great simplicity.

> 16th-century prayer

Keep a green bough within the heart and the singing birds will come.

Chinese proverb

Never miss seeing anything beautiful . . .

Charles Kingsley

Never laugh at live dragons.

J.R. Tolkien, *The Hobbit*

The first rule of education in all lands, is never to say anything offensive to anyone.

Voltaire

Nothing great was ever achieved without enthusiasm.

R.W. Emerson, *Essays*

All work and no play makes Jack a dull boy.

English proverb

~•~

Go placidly amid the noise and haste, and remember what peace there may be in silence. As far as possible, without surrender, be on good terms with all persons. Speak your truth quietly and clearly; and listen to others, even the dull and ignorant; they too have their story.

Avoid loud and aggressive persons, they are vexations to the spirit. If you compare yourself with others, you may become vain and bitter; for always there will be greater and lesser persons than yourself. Enjoy your achievements as well as your plans.

Keep interested in your own career, however humble; it is a real possession in the changing fortunes of time. Exercise caution in your business affairs; for the world is full of trickery. But let this not blind you to what virtue there is, many persons strive for high ideals; and everywhere life is full of heroism.

Anon

Work is the grand cure of all the maladies that ever test mankind.

Thomas Carlyle, speech at Edinburgh University,
2 April 1886

It sorts not, believe me, with wisdom to say "I shall live." Too late is tomorrow's life; live thou to-day.

Martial, *Epigrams*

To fill the hour – that is happiness.

R.W. Emerson, *Essays*

Never put off till tomorrow what you can do today.

English proverb

Speak the truth. Think of others. Don't dawdle.

> Field Marshal Sir William Robertson, at a
> school prize-giving

If at first you don't succeed, try, try again. Then quit. No use being a damn fool about it.

> W.C. Fields (attrib.)

We are always getting ready to live, but never living.

> R.W. Emerson, *Journals*

Toleration is a necessary consequence of our being human. We are all products of frailty – fallible and prone to error – so let us mutually pardon each other's follies. This is the first principle of all human rights.

> Voltaire

A man should never be ashamed to own he has been in the wrong, which is but saying, in other words, that he is wiser today than he was yesterday.

Jonathan Swift, *Time and Tide*

An apple a day keeps the doctor away.

English proverb

One has to resign oneself to being a nuisance if one wants to get anything done.

Freya Stark

You know more than you think you do.

Dr Benjamin Spock, *Commonsense Book of Baby and Child Care*

Nobody is despised by other people unless he has first lost his respect for himself.

Seneca

Never contradict
Never explain
Never apologize
(Those are the secrets of a happy life!)
Admiral Sir John [later Lord] Fisher, letter to
The Times, 5 Sept. 1919

If you want to be happy for a day, get drunk. If you want to be happy for a week, get married. If you want to be happy for life, become a gardener.

Chinese proverb

A house unkept cannot be so distressing as a life unlived.

Rose Macaulay

Life is a mirror: if you frown at it, it frowns back; if you smile, it returns the greeting.

William Makepeace Thackeray

Count your blessings.

English proverb

A man must make his opportunity, as oft as find it.

Francis Bacon, *Advancement of Learning*

Of all human follies there's none could be greater
Than trying to render our fellow-men better.

Molière, *Le Misanthrope*

∼❧∼

The great source of pleasure is variety.

Dr Johnson, *Lives of the English Poets*

∼❧∼

Always dress slowly when you are in a hurry.

Talleyrand

∼❧∼

The password is fortitude.

Violet Needham, *The Black Riders*

∼❧∼

When a person tells you, "I'll think it over and let you know" – you know.

Olin Miller

It's dogged as does it. It ain't thinking about it.
Anthony Trollope, *The Last Chronicle of Barset*

You've got to ac-cent-tchu-ate the
Positive . . .
Johnny Mercer, *"Ac-cent-tchu-ate the Positive"*
(song, music by Harold Arlen)

Practice makes perfect.

English proverb

Conscience is that inner voice that warns us someone
may be looking.
H.L. Mencken, *Little Book in C major*

Sound, sound the clarion, fill the fife,
Throughout the sensual world proclaim,
One crowded hour of glorious life
Is worth an age without a name.

> Thomas Oswald Mordaunt, *Verses Written
> during the War, 1756–63*

The reward of a thing well done, is to have done it.

> R.W. Emerson, *Essays*

Many a man has slept on the Embankment through
not drawing out trumps first.

> Anon, on playing bridge

I have heard with admiring submission the experience of a lady who declares that the sense of being well-dressed gives a feeling of inward tranquillity which religion is powerless to bestow.

R.W. Emerson, *Letters and Social Aims*

Be aisy, and if you can't be aisy,
be as aisy as you can.

Irish proverb

Several excuses are always less convincing than one.

Aldous Huxley, *Point Counter Point*

The most certain sign of wisdom is a continual cheerfulness.

Montaigne, *Essays*

Be not too wise, nor too foolish,
Be not conceited, nor diffident,
Be not haughty, nor too humble,
Be not too talkative, nor too silent,
Be not too hard, nor too feeble.
If you be too wise, men will expect too much of you;
If you be too conceited, you will be thought vexatious;
If you be too humble, you will be without honour;
If you be too talkative, you will not be heeded;
If you be too silent, you will not be regarded;
If you be too hard, you will be broken;
If you be too feeble, you will be crushed.

Instructions of King Cormac
(translated from the Irish)

Men fail much oftener from want of perseverance
than from want of talent.

William Cobbett

No act of kindnesss, however small, is ever in vain.

St Teresa

Work first. Inspiration later.

Igor Stravinsky

Next to knowing when to seize an opportunity, the most important thing in life is to know when to forgo an advantage.

Benjamin Disraeli

Much better not.

Maxim of the 8th Duke of Devonshire

The greatest pleasure I know, is to do a good action by stealth, and have it found out by accident.

Charles Lamb, *Table Talk by the late Elia*,
The Athenaeum, 1834

~·*·~

To read, to think, to love, to hope, to pray, these are the things that make men happy.

Thomas Carlyle

~·*·~

Of making many books there is no end; and much study is a weariness of the flesh.

Bible, Ecclesiastes

~·*·~

There are two times in a man's life when he should not speculate: when he can't afford it, and when he can.

Mark Twain, *Following the Equator*

Bis dat qui cito dat
(He who gives without hesitation gives twice as much)
Publilius Syrus, *Sententiae*

Money is like muck, not good except it be spread.
Francis Bacon, *Essays*

Mind your till and till your mind.
Charles Spurgeon, *Salt Cellars*

Work yourself hard, but not as if you were being made
a victim, and not with any desire for sympathy or
admiration.

Marcus Aurelius, *Meditations*

What is the use of saying that "Many hands make light work" when the same copybook tells you that "Too many cooks spoil the broth"?

Observer, 11 Feb. 1923

Be not righteous overmuch.

Bible, Ecclesiastes

Continual eloquence is tedious.

Blaise Pascal, *Pensées*

Simple rules for saving money: To save half, when you are fired by an eager impulse to contribute to a charity, wait, and count forty. To save three-quarters, count sixty. To save it all, count sixty-five.

Mark Twain, *Following the Equator*

Before doing someone a favour, make sure that he isn't a madman.

Eugène Labiche, *Le Voyage de M. Perrichon*

You should make a point of trying everything in life once, except incest and folk dancing.

Anon

The only place where success comes before work is in a dictionary.

Vidal Sassoon

A journey of a thousand miles starts with one step.

Arab proverb in Primrose Arnander and Ashkhain Skipwith's *The Son of a Duck is a Floater*

Let us not be too particular. It is better to have old second-hand diamonds than none at all.

Mark Twain, *Following the Equator*

Annual income twenty pounds, annual expenditure nineteen nineteen six, result happiness. Annual income twenty pounds, annual expenditure twenty pounds ought and six, result misery.

Mr Micawber in Charles Dickens' *David Copperfield*

Many a mickle makes a muckle.

Scottish proverb

Accustom yourself to give careful attention to what others are saying, and try your best to enter into the mind of the speaker.

Marcus Aurelius, *Meditations*

A little sincerity is a dangerous thing, and a great deal of it is fatal.

Oscar Wilde, *The Critic as Artist*

Our deeds still travel with us from afar,
And what we have been makes us what we are.

George Eliot, *Middlemarch*

I need less WEEK and more WEEKEND.

Anon

Give your decisions, never your reasons; your decisions may be right, but your reasons are sure to be wrong.

William Murray, Earl of Mansfield, *Advice*

Travel light and you can sing in the robber's face.

Juvenal, *Satires*

More people are flattered out of virtue than bullied into vice.

Robert Smith Surtees, *The Analysis of the Hunting Field*

If it ain't broke, don't fix it.

Anon

Caveat emptor.
(Beware the seller.)

Anon

Winners never quit, and quitters never win.

Sarah Paretsky, *V.I. for Short*

Possessions lost, something lost;
Honour lost, much lost;
Courage lost, everything lost.

Johann Wolfgang von Goethe

A man ought to read just as inclination lends him,
for what he reads as a task can do him little good.

Dr Johnson, letter to Boswell, 14 July 1763

Do the duty which lies nearest thee which thou
knowest to be a duty. Thy second duty will already
have become clearer.

Thomas Carlyle, *Past and Present*

Little deeds of kindness, little words of love
Help to make earth happy, like the
Heaven above.

Julia Carney, *Little Things*

Virtue is its own reward.

Anon

Accidents will happen in the best-regulated families.
Mr Micawber in Charles Dickens' *David Copperfield*

A moment on the lips
A lifetime on the hips.

Anon

Do all the good you can,
By all the means you can,
In all the ways you can,
In all the places you can,
At all the times you can,
To all the people you can,
As long as ever you can.

John Wesley, *Rules of Conduct*

You can't make a silk purse out of a sow's ear.

English proverb

Neither a borrower or a lender be
For loan oft loses both itself and friend.

William Shakespeare, *Hamlet*

One smart hat on the head is worth a degree in fashion history.

Edna Woolman Chase, *Vogue*

~❧~

If you want to get ahead, get a hat.

Anon

~❧~

Only a fool would make the bed every day.

Nancy Spain

~❧~

Who goes a borrowing
Goeth a sorrowing
Few lend (but fools)
Their working tools.

Thomas Tusser, *September's Abstract*

Poverty is no disgrace to a man,
But it is confoundedly inconvenient.

Sydney Smith, *His Wit and Wisdom*

~·❧·~

One can never be too thin or too rich.

Wallis Simpson

~·❧·~

The shortest way to do many things is to do only one
thing at once.

Samuel Smiles, *Self Help*

~·❧·~

It was a high counsel that I once heard given to a
young person, "Always do what you are afraid to do."

R.W. Emerson, *Essays*

If you are idle, be not solitary; if you are solitary be not idle.

Dr Johnson, letter to Boswell, 27 Oct. 1779

Never lend books for no one ever returns them; the only books I have in my library are those that other people have lent me.

Anatole France, *La Vie Littéraire*

If you can keep your head when all around you are losing theirs
And blaming it on you . . .
you are gravely underestimating the situation.

Anon

Strike while the iron is hot.

English proverb

Live beyond your means, travel for pleasure, follow your own nose.

W.H. Auden (attrib.)

Judge not, and ye shall not be judged: condemn not, and ye shall not be condemned: forgive, and ye shall be forgiven.

Bible, St Luke

Be a reformer, but don't be found out.

Benjamin Jowett

The cat which isn't let out of the bag often becomes a skeleton in the cupboard.

Geoffrey Madan, *Notebooks*

~·~

Overwork tires; underwork wearies.

Balfour Browne

~·~

It is not possible for a man to be elegant without a touch of femininity.

Vivienne Westwood, *Independent*, 12 July 1990

~·~

To do much good, you must be a very able and patient man: and a bit of a rogue, too: and a good sort of roguery is, never to say a word against anyone, however well deserved.

Benjamin Jowett

In all life one should comfort the afflicted, but verily, also, one should afflict the comfortable, and especially when they are comfortably, contentedly, even happily wrong.

J.K. Galbraith, *Guardian*, 28 July 1989

Walk groundly, talk profoundly, drink roundly, sleep soundly.

William Hazlitt, *English Proverbs*

Success makes life easier. It doesn't make *living* easier.

Bruce Springsteen, *Q Magazine*, Aug. 1992

There is no such thing as a great talent without great will-power.

Honoré de Balzac, *La Muse du Département*

Don't expect too much: and don't attempt too little.

Benjamin Jowett

Never eat anything in one sitting that you can't lift.

Miss Piggy, *Miss Piggy's Guide to Life*

House-keeping ain't no joke.

Louisa May Alcott, *Little Women*

The way to get things done is not to mind who gets the credit of doing them.

Benjamin Jowett

My rule was to do the business of the day on the day.

Duke of Wellington, *Conversations with Stanhope*

Never do today what you can put off till tomorrow.

Punch

If you wish to understand the present look to your past behaviour, if you wish to predict the future, look to your present action.

The Buddha (attrib.)

You'll never plough a field by turning it over in your mind.

Irish proverb

Use a little wine for thy stomach's sake and thine often infirmities.

Bible, I Timothy

A scholar's ink lasts longer than a martyr's blood.

Irish proverb

He who wants to do good knocks at the gate; he who loves finds the door open.

Tagore, *Stray Birds*

It would pay us better to let ourselves be seen as we are than to try to appear what we are not.

Duc de la Rochefoucauld, *Maxims*

One thing I have learned in my wandering life, my friends, is never to call anything a misfortune till you have seen the end of it. Is not every hour a fresh point of view?

Arthur Conan Doyle, *Exploits of Brigadier Gerard*

Study to be quiet, and to do your own business.

Bible, I Thessalonians

Put from you the belief that "I have been wronged" and with it will go the feeling. Reject your sense of injury, and the injury itself disappears.

Marcus Aurelius, *Meditations*

People wish to be settled: only as far as they are unsettled is there any hope for them.

R.W. Emerson, *Essays*

One should always be a little improbable.

Oscar Wilde, *Phrases and Philosophies for the Use of the Young*

Take courage. Some things you will think of for yourself. Others a god will put into your heart.

Homer, *Odyssey*

Be Good. If You Can't Be Good, Be Careful!

Song title, music by James W. Tate

It is easier to be wise for others than for oneself.
Duc de la Rochefoucauld, *Maxims*

Life's too short to stuff a mushroom.
Shirley Conran, *Superwoman*

He that attempts the impossible will often achieve the extremely difficult.
Henry Mackenzie, *The Man of the World*

If a lump of soot falls into the soup, and you cannot conveniently get it out, stir it well in, and it will give the soup a high French taste.
Jonathan Swift, *Advice to Servants*

There's no problem so big or complicated that it can't be run away from.

Graffito, London, 1979

Promises and pie-crust are made to be broken.

Jonathan Swift, *Polite Conversation*

Too feeble fall the impressions of nature to make us artists. Every touch should thrill. Every man should be so much an artist that he could report in conversation what had befallen him.

William Emerson

Unless one is a genius, it is best to aim at being intelligible.

Anthony Hope, *The Dolly Dialogues*

Thou shalt not steal; an empty feat,
When it's so lucrative to cheat.

A.H. Clough, from *"The Latest Decalogue"*

The great business of life is, to be, to do, to do without, and to depart.

John Morley, *Address on Aphorisms*

The great secret in life . . . not to open your letters for a fortnight. At the expiration of that period you will find that nearly all of them have answered themselves.

Arthur Binstead, *Pitcher's Proverbs*

One should always have one's boots on, and be ready to leave.

Montaigne, *Essays*

I get into bed, turn out the light, say "Bugger the lot of them" and go to sleep.

Winston Churchill (attrib.)

Chapter 2

THOUGHTS ON POLITICS

Politicians are the same all over. They promise
to build a bridge even when there's no river.
  Nikita Krushchev, remark at Glen Cove, New
York, 1960

I never trust a man until I've got his pecker in
my pocket.
                    Lyndon Baines Johnson (attrib.)

*What makes a person of power? Are they ever wise? Here
are some answers from the past and present.*

We hold these truths to be sacred and undeniable; that all men are created equal and independent, that from that equal creation they derive rights inherent and inalienable, among which are the preservation of life, and liberty, and the pursuit of happiness.

Thomas Jefferson, Rough draft of the American Declaration of Independence

That all men would be brothers is the dream of people who have no brothers.

Charles Chincholles, *Pensées de tout le monde*

The rain it raineth every day
Upon the just and unjust fella,
But mostly on the just because
The unjust has the just's umbrella.

Anon

The greatest happiness of the greatest number is the foundation of morals and legislation.

Jeremy Bentham, *The Commonplace Book*

Socialism is when you have two cows and give one to your neighbour.

Communism is when you have two cows and the state takes both and gives you milk.

Fascism is when you have two cows and the state takes both and sells you milk.

Nazism is when you have two cows and the state takes both and shoots you.

Capitalism is when you have two cows, sell one and buy a bull.

Bureaucracy is when you have two cows and the state takes both, shoots one, milks the other and pours the milk down the drain.

John J. Quin

Vain hope to make men happy by politics!

Thomas Carlyle, *Journal*

Politics – the gentle art of getting votes from the poor and campaign funds from the rich, by promising to protect each from the other.

Oscar Ameringer

Now, we may say that the most important subjects about which all men deliberate and deliberative orators harangue, are five in number, to wit: ways and means, war and peace, the defence of the country, imports and exports, legislation.

Aristotle, *The Art of Rhetoric*

There is only one step from the sublime to the ridiculous.

> Napoleon I after the retreat from Moscow in 1812,
> in *Histoire de l'Ambassade dans le grand-duché de Varsovie en 1812* by De Pradt

You can fool all the people some of the time, and some of the people all the time, but you cannot fool all the people all the time.

> Abraham Lincoln, speech, 2 Sept. 1858

Men destined to the highest places should beware of badinage.

> Benjamin Disraeli

A politician is a man who understands government and it takes a politician to run a government. A statesman is a politician who's been dead ten or fifteen years.

Harry S. Truman, New York World Telegram and Sun, 12 April 1958

It is my settled opinion, after some years as a political correspondent, that no one is attracted to a political career in the first place unless he is socially or emotionally crippled.

Auberon Waugh, in Richard Reeves' A Ford, not a Lincoln

Nothing appears more surprising to those who consider human affairs with a philosophical eye, than the easiness with which the many are governed by the few.

David Hume, Essays

No Government can be long secure without a formidable Opposition.

Benjamin Disraeli, *Coningsby*

If experience teaches us anything at all, it teaches us this: that a good politician, under democracy, is quite as unthinkable as an honest burglar.

H.L. Mencken, *Prejudices*

Whenever you have an efficient government, you have a dictatorship.

Harry S. Truman, speech, 28 April 1959

The system of good government is to neglect the virtuous and abolish the wise.

Lord Shang, *The Book of Lord Shang*

When security and equality are in conflict, it will not do to hesitate a moment. Equality must yield.

Jeremy Bentham, *Principles of Legislation*

A man may build himself a throne of bayonets, but he cannot sit on it.

William Ralph Inge, *The Wit and Wisdom of Dean Inge*

Our will is always for our own good, but we do not always see what that is.

Jean Jacques Rousseau, *The Social Contract*

In the Lower House, "Don Juan" may perhaps be our model: in the Upper House, "Paradise Lost".

Benjamin Disraeli

A State which dwarfs its men, in order that they may be more docile instruments in its hands even for beneficial purposes – will find that with small men no great thing can really be accomplished.

John Stuart Mill, *Liberty*

You cannot bring about prosperity by discouraging thrift. You cannot strengthen the weak by weakening the strong. You cannot help the wage earner by pulling down the wage payer. You cannot further the brotherhood of man by encouraging class hatred. You cannot help the poor by destroying the rich. You cannot keep out of trouble by spending more than you earn. You cannot build character and courage by taking away man's initiative and independence. You cannot help men permanently by doing for them what they could and should do for themselves.

Abraham Lincoln

Great Actions are not always true sons
Of great and mighty resolutions.

> Samuel Butler, from *"Hudibras"*

Liberty means responsibility. That is why most men
dread it.

> Bernard Shaw, *Maxims for Revolutionists*

Universal suffrage is like the government of a house
by its nursery. But you can do anything with children
if you only play with them.

> Otto von Bismarck

Government, even in its best state, is but a necessary
evil; in its worst state, an intolerable one.

> Thomas Paine, *Common Sense*

When smashing monuments, save the pedestals –
they always come in handy.

Stanislaw Lec, *Unkempt Thoughts*

Whenever our neighbour's house is on fire, it cannot
be amiss for the engines to play a little on our own.

Edmund Burke, *Reflections on the
Revolution in France*

"It is always best on these occasions to do what the
mob do." – "But suppose there are two mobs?"
suggested Mr Snodgras – "Shout with the largest,"
replied Mr Pickwick.

Charles Dickens, *Pickwick Papers*

Conformity is the jailer of freedom and the enemy of growth.

John F. Kennedy, speech, 25 Sept. 1961

A man is not as big as his belief in himself; he is as big as the number of persons who believe in him.

Woodrow Wilson, speech, 3 Oct. 1912

The liberty of the individual must be thus far limited; he must not make himself a nuisance to other people.

John Stuart Mill, *Liberty*

Increased means and increased leisure are the two civilisers of man.

Benjamin Disraeli, speech, 3 April 1872

There is a tide in the affairs of man
Which, taken at the flood, leads on to fortune;
Omitted, all the voyage of their life
Is bound in shallows and in miseries.

William Shakespeare, *Julius Caesar*

The most successful politician is he who says what everybody is thinking most often and in the loudest voice.

Theodore Roosevelt

Those who wish to succeed must ask the right preliminary questions.

Aristotle, *Metaphysics*

Political ability is the ability to foretell what is going to happen tomorrow, next week, next month and next year. And to have the ability afterward to explain why it didn't happen.

Winston Churchill, in B. Adler's *Churchill, Wit*

Prophecy is the most gratuitous form of error.

George Eliot, *Middlemarch*

The empty vessel makes the greatest sound.

English proverb

A prince who desires to maintain his position must learn to be not always good, but to be so or not as needs may require.

Machiavelli, *The Prince*

Circumstances determine our lives, but we shape our lives by what we make of circumstances.

Sir John Wheeler Bennett

When a man assumes a public trust, he should consider himself as public property.

Thomas Jefferson

Politics are now nothing more than a means of rising in the world.

Dr Johnson, in Boswell's *Life of Johnson*

The one thing sure about politics is that what goes up comes down and what goes down often comes up.

Richard Nixon, in Earl Mazo's *Richard Nixon*

If a man hasn't discovered something that he will die for, he isn't fit to live.

Martin Luther King Jr, speech, 23 Jan. 1963

Unlucky the country that needs a hero.

Bertolt Brecht, *Leben des Galilei*

I sit on a man's back, choking him and making him carry me, and yet assure myself and others that I am very sorry for him and wish to ease his lot by all possible means – except by getting off his back.

Leo Tolstoy, *What Then Must We Do?*

When you get to the end of your rope, tie a knot and hang on.

Franklin D. Roosevelt

Reason may be the lever, but sentiment gives you the fulcrum and the place to stand on if you want to move the world.

Oliver Wendell Holmes, *The Poet at the Breakfast Table*

Speech has been given to man to hide his thoughts.

R.P. Malagrida

There is a great deal of hard lying in the world: especially among people whose characters are above suspicion.

Benjamin Jowett

The inquiry of truth, which is the love-making, or wooing of it, the knowledge of truth, which is the presence of it, and the belief of truth, which is the enjoying of it, is the sovereign good of human nature.

Francis Bacon, *Essays*

In statesmanship get the formalities right, never mind about the moralities.

Mark Twain, *Following the Equator*

No man is prejudiced in favour of a thing knowing it to be wrong. He is attached to it in the belief of its being right.

Thomas Paine, *The Rights of Man*

The first requirement of politics is not intellect or stamina but patience. Politics is a very long-run game and the tortoise will usually beat the hare.

John Major, *Daily Express*, 25 July 1989

The greatest thing in the world is to know how to be on one's own.

Montaigne, *Essays*

The most persistent sound which reverberates through man's history is the beating of war drums.

Arthur Koestler, *Janus: A Summing Up*

A very great man once said you should love your enemies, and that's not a bad piece of advice. We can love them, but, by God, that doesn't mean we're not going to fight them.

Norman Schwarzkopf, *Daily Telegraph*,
1 Feb. 1991

Gratitude, like love, is never a dependable international emotion.

Joseph Alsop

Man is only a reed, the weakest thing in nature; but he is a thinking reed.

Blaise Pascal, *Pensées*

Since wars begin in the minds of men, it is in the minds of men that the defence of peace must be constructed.

First lines of the UNESCO charter

To say that man is a reasoning animal is a poetical extravagance.

Arnold Bennett

Man has been endowed with reason, with the power to create, so that he can add to what he's been given. But up to now he hasn't been a creator, only a destroyer. Forests keep disappearing, rivers dry up, wild life's become extinct, the climate's ruined and the land grows poorer and uglier every day.

Anton Chekhov, *Uncle Vanya*

There never was a good war, or a bad peace.
Benjamin Franklin, letter to Quincy,
11 Sept. 1783

~·{·~

We make war that we may live in peace.
Aristotle, *Nicomachean Ethics*

~·{·~

To win a hundred victories in a hundred battles is not the acme of skill. To subdue the enemy without fighting is the supreme excellence.
Sun Tzu, *The Art of War*

~·{·~

Never a day passes over the earth, but men and women of no note do great deeds, speak great words and suffer noble sorrows.
Charles Reade, *The Cloister and the Hearth*

Force and fraud, are in war two cardinal virtues.
Thomas Hobbes, *Leviathan*

Never give out while there is hope; but hope not beyond reason, for that shows more desire than judgement.
William Penn, *Some Fruits of Solitude*

To jaw-jaw is always better than to war-war.
Winston Churchill, speech at the White House,
June 1954

The various opinions of philosophers have scattered through the world as many plagues of the mind as Pandora's box did those of the body; only with this difference, that they have not left hope at the bottom.

Jonathan Swift, *A Critical Essay upon the Faculties of the Mind*

When will the world know that peace and propagation are the two most delightful things in it?

Horace Walpole, 4th Earl of Orford, letter to Sir Horace Mann, 7 July 1778

Most people prefer the existence of a problem which they cannot explain, to an explanation of it which they cannot understand.

Arthur Balfour

The real question (of evil) is presented by those who do vile things for ideal reasons.

Oswald Mosley, *My Life*

It is necessary only for the good man to do nothing for evil to triumph.

Edmund Burke (attrib.)

We will have to repent in this generation not merely for the hateful words and actions of the bad people but for the appalling silence of the good people.

Martin Luther King Jr, *Why We Can't Wait*

Good men must not obey the laws too well.

R.W. Emerson, *Politics*

Truth exists: only lies are invented.

> Georges Braque, *Pensées sur l'art*

<hr>

The broad masses of the people . . . will more easily fall victims to a big lie than to a small one.

> Adolf Hitler, *Mein Kampf*

<hr>

A lie can be half-way round the world before truth has got its boots on.

> James Callaghan, speech, 1 Nov. 1976,
> quoting a proverb

<hr>

When words lose their meaning, people lose their freedom.

> Confucius

Whoever can conquer the street will one day conquer the state, for every form of power politics and any dictatorially-run state has its roots in the street.

Joseph Goebbels, Nazi party congress, Aug. 1927

Freedom of the press is guaranteed only to those who own one.

A.J. Liebling, *The Wayward Press: Do you belong in Journalism?*

Words are like leaves; and where they most abound,
Much fruit of sense beneath is rarely found.

Alexander Pope, from *"An Essay on Criticism"*

Top politicians generally have an arm's length acquaintance with their own language: they only truly mean what other people help them say.

Julian Barnes, on Margaret Thatcher's memoirs, in *Letters from London*

There are three kinds of lies: lies, damned lies, and statistics.

Benjamin Disraeli (attrib.)

One cool judgement is worth a thousand hasty counsels. The thing to be supplied is light, not heat.

Woodrow Wilson, speech, 29 Jan. 1916

Truth is the most valuable thing we have. Let us economize it.

Mark Twain, Following the Equator

Nothing is more dangerous than an idea, when it's the only one we have.

Emile Auguste Chartier, La Lumière

A falsehood mixed with expediency is better than a truth that stirs trouble.

Sa'adi (Persian poet)

On a huge hill,
Cragged and steep, Truth stands, and he that will
Reach her, about must, and about must go.

John Donne, from "Satire no. 3"

The truth is rarely pure, and never simple.
Oscar Wilde, *The Importance of Being Earnest*

Political language . . . is designed to make lies sound truthful and murder respectable and to give an appearance of solidity to pure wind.
George Orwell, *"Politics and the English Language"*

Some things stay there, some things go out of the other ear, and some things don't go in at all.
Elizabeth II, on her regular audiences with prime ministers, *Guardian,* 20 April 1996

Speech is often barren; but silence also does not necessarily brood over a full nest.
George Eliot, *Felix Holt*

In the kingdom of the blind, the one-eyed man is king.

Erasmus, *Adages*

~§~

Success reveals infirmities which failure would otherwise conceal.

John Stuart Mill, *On Liberty*

~§~

Extreme hopes are born of extreme misery.

Bertrand Russell, *Unpopular Essays*

~§~

The world has always gone through periods of madness so as to advance a bit on the road to reason.

Hermann Broch, *The Spell*

The philosophers, cloaked and bearded to command respect, insist that they alone have wisdom and all other mortals are but fleeting shadows. Theirs is certainly a pleasant form of madness, which sets them building countless universes.

Erasmus, *In Praise of Folly*

Experience is the father of wisdom, and memory the mother.

S. Guazzo, *Civil Conversation 1*

What experience and history teach is this – that people and governments never have learned anything from history, or acted on principles deduced from it.

G.W.F. Hegel, *Philosophy of History*

When we got into office, the thing that surprised me most was to find that things were just as bad as we'd been saying they were.

> John F. Kennedy, speech on his 44th birthday,
> 27 May 1961

Only the insane take themselves seriously.

> Max Beerbohm, quoted in *Max* by Lord David Cecil

One of the extraordinary things about human events is that the unthinkable becomes thinkable.

> Salman Rushdie, *Guardian*, 8 Nov. 1990

It appears always easier to recognize inhumanity when it lies on someone else's doorstep.

> Mahatma Gandhi

The greatest evil that one has to fight constantly, every minute of the day until one dies, is the worse part of oneself.

Patrick McGoohan

Nothing is irreparable in politics.

Jean Anouilh, *The Lark*

At bottom, every state regards another as a gang of robbers who will fall upon it as soon as there is an opportunity.

Schopenhauer, *Parerga and Paralipomena*

Politics is just like show business, you have a hell of an opening, coast for a while, and then have a hell of a close.

Ronald Reagan, to Stuart Spencer (aide), 1966

Fame and tranquillity can never be bedfellows.

Montaigne, *Essays*

For forms of government let fools contest;
Whate'er is best administered is best:
For modes of faith let graceless zealots fight
His can't be wrong whose life is in the right:
In faith and hope the world will disagree
But all mankind's concern is charity.

Alexander Pope, from *"An Essay on Man"*

A man always has two reasons for what he does – a good one, and the real one.

J.P. Morgan (attrib.) in Owen Wister's *Roosevelt: The Story of a Friendship*

Unless a man feels he has a good enough memory, he should never venture to lie.

Montaigne, *Essays*

By three things is the world preserved: by truth, by judgement, and by peace . . . The three are really one; if judgement is executed, truth is vindicated and peace results.

Mishnah, *Abothm*

I think politics is an instrument of the devil.
Bob Dylan, interview in *Rolling Stone*

Great men are but life-sized. Most of them, indeed, are rather short.

Max Beerbohm, *And Even Now*

Chapter 3

FRIENDS AND SOCIETY

Love and scandal are the best sweeteners of tea.
Henry Fielding, *Love in Several Masques*

Strange to see how a good dinner and feasting
reconciles everybody.
Samuel Pepys, *Diary*, 9 Nov. 1665

*How to make friends, and how to keep them; how to
forgive, if not to forget; what your friends really want of
you, what you can demand of them; how to be a good host,
or a bad guest; how, as Bacon put it, to be "a citizen of the
world."*

The sun has risen twice today.

Chinese greeting on meeting someone
unexpectedly

~·{≈·~

Sir, I look upon every day to be lost, in which I do not
make a new acquaintance.

Dr Johnson, in Boswell's *Life of Johnson*

~·{≈·~

He may live without books – what is knowledge but
  grieving?
He may live without hope – what is hope but
  deceiving?
He may live without love – what is passion but
  pining?
But where is the man that can live without dining?

Owen Meredith (Edward Robert Bulwer,
Earl of Lytton), from *"Lucile"*

A man hath no better thing under the sun, than to eat, and to drink, and to be merry.

> Bible, Ecclesiastes

≈⟨●⟩≈

He has occasional flashes of silence, that make his conversation perfectly delightful.

> Sydney Smith about Lord Macaulay, in Lady Holland's *Memoir*

≈⟨●⟩≈

Speak in French when you can't think of the English for a thing.

> Lewis Carroll, *Through the Looking-Glass*

≈⟨●⟩≈

And, when you stick on conversation's burrs,
Don't strew your pathway with those dreadful urs.

> Oliver Wendell Holmes, from *"A Rhymed Lesson"*

The re-assurance of habit and the priceless gifts of companionship and conversation.

Richard Cobb, *Death in Paris*

∼⟨●⟩∼

Friendship is a sheltering tree.

Samuel Taylor Coleridge

∼⟨●⟩∼

A man that studieth revenge keeps his own wounds green.

Francis Bacon, *Essays*

∼⟨●⟩∼

To refrain from imitation is the best revenge.

Marcus Aurelius, *Meditations*

The secret of being a bore . . . is to say everything.

Voltaire, *Sept discours en vers sur l'homme*

Compliments always embarrass a man . . . I have been complimented myself a great many times, and they always embarrass me – I always feel that they have not said enough.

Mark Twain, *Speeches*

I suppose flattery hurts no one, that is, if he doesn't inhale.

Adlai Stevenson, television broadcast, 30 March 1952

If a man be gracious and courteous to strangers, it shows he is a citizen of the world.

Francis Bacon, *Essays*

If you think it's hard to meet new people, try picking up the wrong golf ball.
Jack Lemmon, *Sports Illustrated*, 9 Dec. 1985

In vino veritas.

Anon

There is no man so friendless but what he can find a friend sincere enough to tell him disagreeable truths.
Edward George Bulwer-Lytton,
What will he do with it?

When you're smiling the whole world smiles with you.
Goodwin and Shay, from
"When You're Smiling" (song)

Give me the avowed, elect and manly foe;
Firm I can meet, perhaps return the blow,
But of all plagues, good Heaven, thy wrath can send,
Save me, oh, save me, from the candid friend.

George Canning, *New Morality*

Praise is the best diet for us, after all.

Sydney Smith, in Lady Holland's *Memoir*

Clothes make the man. Naked people have little or
no influence in society.

Mark Twain, in *More Maxims of Mark Twain*,
ed. M. Johnson

In prosperity our friends know us; in adversity we know our friends.

Churton Collins, *English Review*

The louder he talked of his honour, the faster we counted our spoons.

R.W. Emerson, *The Conduct of Life*

True friendship is never serene.

Marquise de Sevigné, *Letters*

Never speak ill of yourself, your friends will always say enough on that subject.

Talleyrand

He banked his treasure in the hearts of his friends.
                    Winston Churchill of F.E. Smith

∼✿∼

Unbidden guests
Are often welcomest when they are gone.
                    William Shakespeare, *Henry VI, Part II*

∼✿∼

A good laugh is the best pesticide.
                    Vladimir Nabokov, *Strong Opinions*

∼✿∼

He who has a thousand friends has not a friend to
    spare.
And he who has one enemy will meet him everywhere.
                    Ali Ibn-Abi-Talib, *Sentences*

All our foes are mortal.

Paul Valéry, *Tel Quel*

～•～

There is so much good in the worst of us,
And so much bad in the best of us,
That it hardly becomes any of us
To talk about the rest of us.

Anon

～•～

A faithful friend is the medicine of life.

Apocrypha, Ecclesiasticus

～•～

Friendship is not always the sequel of obligation.

Dr Johnson, *Lives of the English Poets*

What has one to do, when one grows tired of the world, as we both do, but to draw nearer and nearer, and gently waste the remains of life with friends with whom one began it?

Horace Walpole, 4th Earl of Orford, letter to George Montagu, 21 Nov. 1765

The holy passion of Friendship is of so sweet and steady and loyal and enduring a nature that it will last through a whole lifetime, if not asked to lend money.

Mark Twain, *The Tragedy of Pudd'nhead Wilson*

A good book is the best of friends, the same today and forever.

Martin Farquhar Tupper, *Proverbial Philosophy*

Absence is to love what wind is to fire;
It extinguishes the small, it enkindles the great.
Comte de Bussy Rabutin, *Histoire Amoreuse des Gaules*

Between men and women there is no friendship possible. There is passion, enmity, worship, love, but no friendship.
Oscar Wilde, *A Woman of No Importance*

A friend in power is a friend lost.
Henry Adams, *The Education of Henry Adams*

In the misfortunes of our best friends, we find something that is not unpleasing.
Duc de la Rochefoucauld, *Suppressed Maxims*

There is no spectacle more agreeable than to observe an old friend fall from a roof-top.

Confucius

Life is to be fortified by many friendships. To love, and to be loved, is the greatest happiness of existence.

Sydney Smith, in Lady Holland's *Memoir*

It takes two to make a quarrel.

English proverb

If a man does not make new acquaintance as he advances through life, he will soon find himself alone. A man, Sir, should keep his friendships in *constant repair*.

Dr Johnson, in Boswell's *Life of Johnson*

The art of hospitality is to make guests feel at home when you wish they were.

Anon

~·%·~

Good breeding consists in concealing how much we think of ourselves and how little we think of the other person.

Mark Twain, in *Mark Twain's Notebook*, ed. A.B. Paine

~·%·~

Never waste a minute thinking about people you don't like.

Dwight D. Eisenhower

~·%·~

A friend in need is a friend indeed.

English proverb

Whenever a friend succeeds, a little something in me dies.

Gore Vidal, *Sunday Times Magazine*, 1973

Keep your temper. Do not quarrel with an angry person, but give him a soft answer. It is commanded by the Holy Writ and, furthermore, it makes him madder than anything else you could do.

Anon, *Reader's Digest*, 1949

Love is blind; friendship closes its eyes.

Anon

Old friends are best. King James used to ask for his old shoes; they were easiest for his feet.

John Selden, *Table Talk*

I love everything that's old; old friends, old times, old manners, old books, old wines.

Oliver Goldsmith, *She Stoops to Conquer*

Ask only those people to stay with you or to dine with you who can ask you in return.

The Vicar of Whitstable

I am convinced digestion is the great secret of life.

Sydney Smith, letter to Arthur Kinglake, 30 Sept. 1837

Man is the Only Animal that blushes. Or needs to.

Mark Twain, *Following the Equator*

I must decline your invitation owing to a subsequent invitation.

Oscar Wilde

Be civil with all; sociable to many; familiar with few.

Benjamin Disraeli

The ae half of the warld thinks the tither daft.

Walter Scott, *Redgauntlet*

Love makes the world go round? Not at all. Whisky makes it go round twice as fast.

Compton Mackenzie, *Whisky Galore*

The best number for a dinner party is two – myself and a dam' good head waiter.

Nubar Gulbenkian, *Daily Telegraph,* 14 Jan. 1965

~·ﹸ·~

But I'm not so think as you drunk I am.

J.C. (Sir John) Squire, *Ballade of Soporific Absorption*

~·ﹸ·~

It is absurd to divide people into good and bad. People are either charming or tedious.

Oscar Wilde, *Lady Windermere's Fan*

~·ﹸ·~

Bad men live to eat and drink, whereas good men eat and drink in order to live.

Plutarch, *Moralia*

You must come again when you have less time.

Walter Sickert

I've noticed that the people who are late are often so much jollier than the people who have to wait for them.

E.V. Lucas, *365 Days and One More*

Some cause happiness wherever they go; others whenever they go.

Oscar Wilde

A bore is someone who persists in holding his own views after we have enlightened him with ours.

Malcolm L. Forbes

Forsake not an old friend: for the new is not comparable to him: a new friend is as new wine: when it is old, thou shalt drink with pleasure.

Apocrypha, Ecclesiasticus

I believe I once considerably scandalized her by declaring that clear soup was a more important factor in life than a clear conscience.

Saki (H.H. Munro), *The Blind Spot*

Two days y'ave larded here; a third ye know,
Makes guests and fish smell strong, pray go.

Robert Herrick, from *"Hesperides"*

Friendship is constant in all other things
Save in the office and affairs of love.

William Shakespeare, *Much Ado About Nothing*

I have lost friends, some by death . . . others through
sheer inability to cross the street.

> Virginia Woolf, *The Waves*

Appetite comes with eating.

> François Rabelais, *Gargantua*

The cocktail party – a device for paying off
obligations to people you don't want to invite to
dinner.

> Charles Merrill Smith, *Instant Status*

Society, friendship and love,
Divinely bestowed upon man,
Oh, had I the wings of a dove,
How soon would I taste you again.

> William Cowper, from *"Verses supposed to be
> Written by Alexander Selkirk"*

Should auld acquaintance be forgot
And never brought to min'
Should auld acquaintance be forgot,
And days o' lang syne?
. . .
For auld lang syne, my dear,
For auld lang syne,
We'll take a cup o' kindness yet
For auld lang syne.

Robert Burns, *Auld Lang Syne*

We cherish our friends not for their ability to amuse us, but for ours to amuse them.

Evelyn Waugh

That all-softening, overpowering knell,
The tocsin of the soul – the dinner bell.

Byron, from *"Don Juan"*

Tart words make no Friends: a spoonful of honey will catch more flies than a Gallon of Vinegar.

Benjamin Franklin, *Poor Richard's Almanac*

If you cannot mould yourself as you would wish, how can you expect other people to be entirely to your liking.

Thomas à Kempis, *The Imitation of Christ*

Flattery must be pretty thick before anybody objects to it.

William Feather, *The Business of Life*

The flowers of the earth do no grudge at one another, though one be more beautiful and fuller of virtue than another; but they stand kindly one by another, and enjoy one another's virtue.

Jakob Boehme, *The Threefold Life of Man*,
tr. J. Sparrow

One cannot have too large a party. A large party secures its own amusement.

Jane Austen, *Emma*

Manners are especially the need of the plain. The pretty can get away with anything.

Evelyn Waugh, *Observer Sayings of the Year 1962*

A party is like a marriage . . . making itself up while seeming to follow precedent . . .

Jay McInerney, *Brightness Falls*

I always allow other people to be right. It consoles them for not being anything else.

André Gide

A little inaccuracy sometimes saves tons of explanation.

Saki (H.H. Munro), *The Square Egg*

At every party there are two kinds of people – those who want to go home and those who don't. The trouble is, they are usually married to each other.

Ann Landers, *International Herald Tribune,*
19 June 1991

It is true that we are weak and sick and ugly and quarrelsome but if that is all we ever were, we would millenniums ago have disappeared from the face of the earth.

John Steinbeck, in *Writers at Work,*
ed. George Plimpton

What I've learned about being angry with people is that it generally hurts you more than it hurts them.

Oprah Winfrey, in *Oprah!* by Robert Waldron

Though I speak with the tongues of men and of angels, and have not charity, I am become as sounding brass, or a tinkling cymbal.

Bible, I Corinthians

This only is charity, to do all, all that we can.

John Donne

To err is human,
To forgive takes restraint;
To forget you forgave
Is the mark of a saint.

Suzanne Douglass, *Reader's Digest*, 1966

It is a fine thing to forgive your enemies: but it is a finer thing not to be too eager to forgive yourself.

G.K. Chesterton

May you have warm words on a cold evening,
A full moon on a dark night,
And the road downhill all the way to your door.

Irish blessing

Men should always be difficult. I can't bear men who come to dine with you when you want them.

Benjamin Disraeli

No one ever praised two men equally, and pleased them both.

Sir Arthur Helps

To be happy in threes is a great test of the capacity for being happy at all.

Mary Coleridge

Now may every living thing, feeble or strong, omitting none, or tall or middle-sized or short, subtle or gross of form, seen or unseen, those dwelling near or far away – whether they be born or yet unborn – may every living thing be full of bliss.

The Buddha from *Some Sayings of the Buddha,* tr. F.L. Woodward

Time to me this truth has taught
('Tis a treasure worth revealing),
More offend from want of thought,
Than any want of feeling.

Charles Swain, *Want of Thought*

Thoughtless good humour will often make more enemies than deliberate spite . . .

William Hazlitt

Every time I paint a portrait I lose a friend.

John Singer Sargent (attrib.)

Never listen to accounts of the frailties of others; and if anyone should complain to you of another, humbly ask him not to speak about him at all.

St John of the Cross

Be nice to people on your way up, because you'll meet 'em on your way down.

Wilson Mizner, *The Legendary Mizners*

No good story is quite true.

Leslie Stephen, *Life of Milton*

To speak highly of one with whom we are intimate is a form of egotism.

William Hazlitt

Friendships begin with liking or gratitude – roots that can be pulled up.

George Eliot, *Daniel Deronda*

Thou shalt not avenge, nor bear any grudge against the children of thy people, but thou shalt love thy neighbour as thyself ...

Bible, Leviticus

Do not be surprised at the ingratitude of those to whom you have given nothing but money.

Sir Arthur Helps

An indecent mind is a perpetual feast.

Oscar Wilde

~᠁~

Good people are not so good as they imagine; and bad people are not so bad as the good suppose.

Bishop Creighton to Lord Acton

~᠁~

He who laughs last is generally the last to get the joke.

Terry Cohen, in P. and J. Holton's
Quote and Unquote

~᠁~

Every friendship rests on some particular apotheosis of oneself.

F.H. Bradley

Life is mostly froth and bubble,
Two things stand like stone,
Kindness in another's trouble,
Courage in your own.

Adam Lindsay Gordon, from *"Man's Testament"*

Make new friends but keep the old,
One is like silver the other gold.

English proverb

He who would do good to another, must do it in minute particulars.

General good is the plea of the scoundrel, hypocrite, and flatterer.

William Blake, from *Jerusalem*

Every man should keep a fair-sized cemetery in which to bury the faults of his friends.

Henry Ward Beecher

Better is a dinner of herbs where love is, than a stalled ox and hatred therewith.

Bible, Proverbs

This was a good dinner enough, to be sure, but it was not a dinner to *ask* a man to.

Dr Johnson in Boswell's *Life of Johnson*

Gossip is the sort of smoke that comes from the dirty tobacco pipes of those who diffuse it; it proves nothing but the bad taste of the smoker.

George Eliot, *Daniel Deronda*

There is only one thing in the world worse than being talked about, and that is not being talked about.

Oscar Wilde, *The Picture of Dorian Gray*

Men may swallow being cheated, but no man can ever endure to chew it.

Lord Halifax, *Works*

All natural talk is a festival of ostentation; and by the laws of the game each accepts and fans the vanity of the other.

Robert Louis Stevenson, *Memories and Portraits: Talk and Talkers*

There are some people whose good manners will not suffer them to interrupt you, but, what is almost as bad, will discover an abundance of impatience, and lie upon the watch until you have done, because they have started something in their own thoughts, which they long to be delivered of.

Jonathan Swift, *Hints Toward an Essay on Conversation*

~·~

Frankness is the backbone of friendship – when it is covered by the flesh of tact.

C.G. Colmore, *The Angel and the Outcast*

~·~

We never knows wot's hidden in each other's hearts; and if we had glass winders there, we'd need keep the shutters up, some on us, I do assure!

Mrs Gamp in Charles Dickens' *Martin Chuzzlewit*

Always be ready to speak your mind, and a base man will avoid you.

William Blake, *Proverbs of Hell*

Brevity is the soul of wit.

William Shakespeare, *Hamlet*

Brevity is the soul of lingerie.

Dorothy Parker

Don't jump on a man unless he's down.

Finley Peter Dunne, *Mr Dooley Remembers*

Laugh and the world laughs with you;
Weep, and you weep alone;
For the sad old earth must borrow its mirth,
But has trouble enough of its own.

Ella Wheeler Wilcox, Solitude

Greater love hath no man than this, that a man lay down his life for his friends.

Bible, St John

The Athenians do not mind a man being clever, so long as he does not impart his cleverness to others.

Plato

Who knows himself a braggart,
Let him fear this, for it will come to pass
That every braggart shall be found an ass.

William Shakespeare, All's Well That Ends Well

It is only people of importance who can afford to be
dull.

Constance Jones, *The Ten Years Agreement*

We often forgive those who bore us; we cannot
forgive those whom we bore.

Duc de la Rochefoucauld, *Maxims*

The penalty of success is to be bored by the people
one used to snub.

Nancy Astor

A bore is a fellow who opens his mouth and puts his
feats in it.

Henry Ford

We are not to judge the feelings of others by what we might feel in their place. However dark the habitation of the mole to our eyes, yet the animal itself finds the apartment sufficiently lightsome.

Oliver Goldsmith, *The Vicar of Wakefield*

There's no such thing as bad publicity except your own obituary.

Brendan Behan

'Tis an old maxim in the schools,
That flattery's the food of fools;
Yet now and then your men of wit
Will condescend to take a bit.

Jonathan Swift, from *"Cadenus and Vanessa"*

A friend married is a friend lost.

Henrik Ibsen, *Love's Comedy*

Troubles overcome are good to tell.

Yiddish proverb

I do not want people to be very agreeable, as it saves me the trouble of liking them a great deal.

Jane Austen, letter to her sister Cassandra,
24 Dec. 1798

Let brotherly love continue.
Be not forgetful to entertain strangers: for thereby some have entertained angels unawares.

Bible, Hebrews

Chapter 4

LOVE AND MARRIAGE

Love and marriage, love and marriage,
Go together like a horse and carriage.
     Sammy Cahn, *"Love and Marriage"* (song)

A lady's imagination is very rapid; it jumps
from admiration to love, from love to
matrimony in a moment.
     Jane Austen, *Pride and Prejudice*

*Any sort of love, not just the married sort, has its ups and
downs.*

What is bettre than wisdom? Woman. And what is bettre than a good woman? No-thing.

Geoffrey Chaucer, *Canterbury Tales*

What is love? 'tis not hereafter
Present mirth hath present laughter;
What's to come is still unsure;
In delay there lies no plenty:
Then come kiss me, sweet and twenty,
Youth's a stuff will not endure.

William Shakespeare, *Twelfth Night*

The expense is damnable, the pleasure momentary and the position ludicrous.

Lord Chesterfield on sex (attrib.)

Love conquers all things except poverty and toothache.

Mae West

～ﬁ～

Love is a great teacher.

St Augustine

～ﬁ～

The love that moves the sun and the other stars.

Dante, *Paradiso*

～ﬁ～

All love at first, like generous wine,
Ferments and frets until 'tis fine;
But when 'tis settled on the lee,
And from th'impurer matter free,
Becomes the richer still the older,
And proves the pleasanter the colder.

Samuel Butler, *Miscellaneous Thoughts*

Love is the wisdom of the fool and the folly of the wise.

> Dr Johnson in William Cooke's
> *Life of Samuel Foote*

Sudden love takes the longest time to be cured.

> La Bruyère, *Characters*

Who ever loved that loved not at first sight?

> Christopher Marlowe, *Hero and Leander*

'Tis well to be merry and wise,
'Tis well to be honest and true;
'Tis well to be off with the old love,
Before you are on with the new.

> Charles Robert Maturin, *Bertram*

Who loves not woman, wine, and song
Remains a fool his whole life long.

Martin Luther (attrib.)

Remember when you go out with gentlemen never to
take wine. It's exciting enough without.

Dame Alix Meynell's grandmother to her mother

The affection of young ladies is of as rapid growth as
Jack's beanstalk, and reaches up to the sky in a night.

William Makepeace Thackeray, *Vanity Fair*

No, the heart that has truly lov'd never forgets,
But as truly loves on to the close,
As the sun-flower turns on her god,
when he sets,
The same look which she turn'd
when he rose.

Thomas Moore, from *"By that Lake"*

Every man needs two women, a quiet homemaker and
a thrilling nymph.

Iris Murdoch, *The Message to the Planet*

Twenty years of romance makes a woman look like a
ruin; but twenty years of marriage make her
something like a public building.

Oscar Wilde, *A Woman of No Importance*

Many a good hanging prevents a bad marriage.

William Shakespeare, *Twelfth Night*

Next to being married, a girl likes to be crossed in love a little now and then.

Jane Austen, *Pride and Prejudice*

Love is a kind of warfare.

Ovid, *Ars Amatoria*

All's fair in love and war.

English proverb

Though women are angels yet
Wedlock's the devil.

Byron, from *"To Eliza"*

Say what you will, 'tis better to be left than never to
have been loved.

William Congreve, *The Way of the World*

People in love . . . suffer extreme conceptual delu-
sions; the most common of all being that other
people find your condition as thrilling and
eyewatering as you yourselves.

Julian Barnes, *Observer*, 1984

. . . I do not like to have people throw themselves
away; but everybody should marry as soon as they can
do it to advantage.

Jane Austen, *Mansfield Park*

The critical period in matrimony is breakfast-time.

A.P. Herbert, *Uncommon Law*

A man in love is incomplete until he is married. Then he is finished.

Zsa Zsa Gabor, *Newsweek*, 28 March 1960

Men are April when they woo,
December when they wed.

William Shakespeare, *As You Like It*

Daisy, Daisy,
Give me your answer do,
I'm half crazy
All for the love of you.
It won't be a stylish marriage
'Cos I can't afford a carriage,
But you'll look sweet
Upon the seat
Of a bicycle made for two.

Michael, Michael,
This is my answer, dear,
I can't cycle,
Makes me come over queer.
If you can't afford a carriage
Then there won't be a marriage,
For I'll be blowed
If I'll be towed
On a bicycle made for two.

Edwardian music hall song

An engaged woman is always more agreeable than a disengaged. She is satisfied with herself. Her cares are over, and she feels that she may exert all her powers of pleasing without suspicion.

Jane Austen, *Mansfield Park*

[Wedlock] . . . the deep, deep peace of the double-bed after the hurley-burly of the chaise-longue.

Mrs Patrick Campbell, in Alexander Woolcott's
While Rome Burns

Love is blind but marriage restores the sight.

English proverb

It doesn't much signify whom one marries, for one is sure to find next morning that it was someone else.

Samuel Rogers, *Table Talk*

So that is marriage, Lily thought, a man and a woman looking at a girl throwing a ball.

Virginia Woolf, *To the Lighthouse*

When I wanted to go upstairs, there was my wife coming down; or when my wife wanted to go down, there was I coming up. That is married life, according to my experience of it.

Wilkie Collins, *The Moonstone*

The roaring of the wind is my wife and the stars through the window pane are my children.

John Keats, letter to George and Georgiana Keats, 24 Oct. 1818

Jack Sprat could eat no fat
His wife could eat no lean;
And so between them both, you see,
They licked the platter clean.

Nursery rhyme

Marriage is not all bed and breakfast.
R. Coulson, *Reflections*

The husband who wants a happy marriage should learn to keep his mouth shut and his checkbook open.
Groucho Marx

Those who talk most about the blessings of marriage and the constancy of its vows are the very people who declare that if the chain were broken and the prisoners left to choose, the whole social fabric would fly asunder. You cannot have the argument both ways. If the prisoner is happy, why lock him in? If he is not, why pretend that he is?

Bernard Shaw, *Man and Superman*

It [marriage] is like a cage; one sees the birds outside desperate to get in, and those inside equally desperate to get out.

Montaigne, *Essays*

Chains do not hold a marriage together. It is threads, hundreds of tiny threads . . .

Simone Signoret, *Daily Mail*, 4 July 1978

Question: In your long married life, Lady Longford, have you ever contemplated divorce?
Reply: Murder often, divorce never.

Elizabeth Longford to a journalist

. . . my wife and I home and find all well. Only, myself somewhat vexed at my wife's neglect in leaving of her scarfe, waistcoat, and night-dressings in the coach today that brought us from Westminster, though I confess she did give them to me to look after — yet it was her fault not to see that I did take them out of the coach.

Samuel Pepys, *Diary*, 6 Jan. 1663

Husbands, love your wives, and be not bitter against them.

Bible, Colossians

It is proverbial that from a hungry tiger and an affectionate woman there is no escape.

Ernest Bramah, *Kai Lung Unrolls his Mat*

Man's love is of man's life a thing apart,
'Tis woman's whole existence.

Byron, from *"Don Juan"*

Every woman should marry – and no man.

Benjamin Disraeli, *Lothair*

All happy families resemble each other, each unhappy family is unhappy in its own way.

The opening sentence of Leo Tolstoy's
Anna Karenina

What men call gallantry, and gods adultery,
Is much more common where the climate's sultry.

> Byron, from *"Don Juan"*

No man worth having is true to his wife, or can be true to his wife, or ever was, or ever will be so.

> Sir John Vanbrugh, *The Relapse*

O philosopher, you who see nothing save things of the moment, how limited is your vision! Your eyes are not made to follow the underground workings of passion.

> Johann Wolfgang von Goethe

I hate women because they always know where things are.

> James Thurber

Birth and death are natural accidents: marriage we can avoid.

George Meredith, *The Ordeal of Richard Feverel*

Married life is merely a habit, a bad habit. But then one regrets the loss even of one's worse habits. Perhaps one regrets them the most. They are such an essential part of one's personality.

Oscar Wilde, *The Picture of Dorian Gray*

My boy, be wery careful o' widders all your life.

Mr Weller in Charles Dickens' *Pickwick Papers*

Wives are young men's mistresses, companions for middle age, and old men's nurses.

Francis Bacon, *Essays*

Once a woman has given her heart you can never get rid of the rest of her.

Sir John Vanbrugh, *The Relapse*

She who would long retain her power must use her lover ill.

Ovid, *Amores*

They that marry where they do not love, will love where they do not marry.

Thomas Fuller, *The Holy State and the Profane State*

Those who are faithful know only the trivial side of love: it is the faithless who know love's tragedies.

Oscar Wilde, *The Picture of Dorian Gray*

A legal kiss is never as good as a stolen one.

Guy de Maupassant, *A Wife's Confession*

When a man steals your wife, there is no better revenge than to let him keep her.

Sacha Guitry, *Elles et toi*

Sigh no more, ladies, sigh no more
Men were deceivers ever,
One foot on sea, and one on shore
To one thing constant never.
Then leave your woe, and let them go
And be you blithe and bonny,
Forsaking all your grief and woe
To sing hey nonny nonny.

William Shakespeare, *Much Ado about Nothing*

Higamus, hogamus,
Woman is monogamous,
Hogamus, higamus
Man is polygamous.

Anon

What is the conscience but a pair of breeches which, while it serves as a cloak both for lewdness and nastiness, may be readily let down in the service of either?

Jonathan Swift

There is a middle state between love and friendship more delightful than either but more difficult to remain in.

Walter Savage Landor

He that hath wife and children hath given hostages to fortune; for they are impediments to great enterprises, either of virtue or mischief.

Francis Bacon, *Essays*

Love makes time pass;
Time makes love pass.

Italian saying

The grave's a fine and private place,
But none, I think, do there embrace.
Andrew Marvell, from "*To his Coy Mistress*"

A little disdain is not amiss; a little scorn is alluring.
William Congreve, *The Way of the World*

For money has a power above
The stars and fate, to manage love.

Samuel Butler, from *"Hudibras"*

I never hated a man enough to give his diamonds back.

Zsa Zsa Gabor, *Observer sayings of the Week,*
28 Aug. 1959

Marrying for money is the hardest way to get it.

Anon

A gentleman who had been very unhappy in marriage, married immediately after his wife had died: Johnson said it was a triumph of hope over experience.

Dr Johnson in Boswell's *Life of Johnson*

Any man who says he can see through a woman is missing a lot.

Groucho Marx

A man is in general better pleased when he has a good dinner upon his table, than when his wife talks Greek.

Dr Johnson in *Johnson's Works*, ed. Hawkins

She said she always believed in the old adage – leave them while you're looking good.

Anita Loos, *Gentlemen Prefer Blondes*

Were it not for imagination, a man would be as happy
in the arms of a chambermaid as a Duchess.

> Dr Johnson in Boswell's *Life of Johnson*

Ah, love, let us be true
To one another! for the world, which seems
To lie before us like a land of dreams,
So various, so beautiful, so new,
Hath really neither joy, nor love, nor light,
Nor certitude, nor peace, nor help for pain;
And we are here as on a darkling plain
Swept with confused alarms of struggle and flight,
Where ignorant armies clash by night.

> Matthew Arnold, from *"Dover Beach"*

I hate and I love: why I do so you may well ask. I do
not know, but I feel it happen and am in agony.

> Catullus, *Carmina no. 8*

Love rekindled, like a cigar relit, is never the same.

Anon

If ever I marry a wife,
I'll marry a landlord's daughter,
For then I may sit in the bar,
And drink cold brandy and water.

Charles Lamb

Had Cleopatra's nose been shorter the whole history of the world would have been different.

Blaise Pascal, *Pensées*

Women's beauty, like men's wit, is generally fatal to the owners.

Lord Chesterfield, *Miscellaneous Notes*

Love is a growing or full constant light;
And his first minute, after noon, is night.

John Donne, from *"Songs and Sonnets"*

Heroine: girl who is perfectly charming to live with,
in a book.

Mark Twain in *More Maxims of Mark Twain*,
ed. M. Johnson

A difference of taste in jokes is a great strain on the
affections.

George Eliot, *Daniel Deronda*

It is difficult suddenly to lay aside a long cherished
love.

Catullus, *Carmina no. 76*

The hind that would be mated with the lion
Must die of love.
William Shakespeare, *All's Well That Ends Well*

All the privilege I claim for my own sex . . . is that of
loving longest, when existence or when hope is gone.
Jane Austen, *Persuasion*

Bachelors are not fashionable any more. They are a
damaged lot. Too much is known about them.
Oscar Wilde, *An Ideal Husband*

I have always been principally interested in men for sex. I've always thought any sane woman would be a lover of women because loving men is such a mess.

Germaine Greer, *New York Times Book Review*, 11 Oct. 1992

~❧~

Every woman would rather be beautiful than good.

German proverb

~❧~

Chaste is she whom no one has asked.

Ovid, *Amores*

~❧~

I will find you twenty lascivious turtles ere one chaste man.

William Shakespeare, *The Merry Wives of Windsor*

All women marry gods, but sadly consent afterwards to live with men.

Henry Ward Beecher, *Norwood*

If you cannot catch a bird of paradise, better take a wet hen.

Russian proverb

It is a great help for a man to be in love with himself. For an actor, however, it is absolutely essential.

Robert Morley, *Playboy*, 1979

A woman's virtue ought indeed to be great: since it often has to suffice for two.

Queen Marie of Roumania

Love gratified is love satisfied, and love satisfied is indifference begun.

Samuel Richardson

Marriage is like the Middle East. There's no solution.

Pauline Collins, in *Shirley Valentine* (film) by Willy Russell

Girls bored me – they still do. I love Mickey Mouse more than any woman I've ever known.

Walt Disney

Marriage has many pains, but celibacy has no pleasures.

Dr Johnson, *Rasselas*

Rituals are important. Nowadays it's hip not to be married. I'm not interested in being hip.

John Lennon, *Playboy,* Sept. 1980

Between husband and wife a shadow of courtship should always subsist.

Queen Marie of Roumania

Where there is no love there is no sense either.

Fyodor Dostoevsky, *Notes from Underground*

Bourgeois marriage is in reality a system of wives in common . . .

Karl Marx, *Communist Manifesto*

Contraceptives should be used on every conceivable occasion.

Spike Milligan, *The Last Goon Show of Them All*

Fear not, sweet love, what time can do;
Though silver dims the gold
Of your soft hair, believe that you
Can change but not grow old.

Though since we married thirty years
And four have flown away,
As bright your beauty still appears
As on our wedding day.

We will not weep that spring be past
And autumn shadows fall;
These years shall be, although the last,
The loveliest of all.

Alfred Duff Cooper, *"To Diana,"*
dedication to *Old Men Forget*

Affection may now and then withstand very severe storms of rigor, but not a long polar frost of downright indifference.

Walter Scott, *Waverley*

Love consists in this, that two solitudes protect and border and salute each other.

Rainer Maria Rilke, *Letters to a Young Poet*

Yet if you should forget me for a while
And afterwards remember, do not grieve:
For if the darkness and corruption leave
A vestige of the thoughts that once I had,
Better by far you should forget and smile
Than that you should remember and be sad.

Christina Rossetti, from "*Remember*"

To live in hearts we leave behind
Is not to die.

> Thomas Campbell, from *"Hallowed Ground"*

Love made me poet,
And this I writ;
My heart did do it,
And not my wit.

> Elizabeth, Lady Tanfield, epitaph for her husband

Change everything except your loves.

> Voltaire, *Sur l'Usage de la Vie*

Adieu to disappointment and spleen. What are men to rocks and mountains?

> Jane Austen, *Pride and Prejudice*

Heav'n has no rage, like love to hatred turn'd,
Nor Hell a fury, like a woman scorn'd.

William Congreve, *The Mourning Bride*

It is poverty only which makes celibacy contemptible to a generous public! A single woman, with a very narrow income, must be a ridiculous, disagreeable, old maid! The proper sport of boys and girls; but a single woman, of good fortune, is always respectable, and may be as sensible and pleasant as anybody else.

Jane Austen, *Emma*

The happiest women, like the happiest nations, have no history.

George Eliot, *The Mill on the Floss*

For this is Wisdom; to love, to live,
To take what Fate, or the Gods may give,
To ask no question, to make no prayer,
But to kiss the lips and caress the hair,
Speed passion's ebb as you greet its flow, –
To have, – to hold, and, – in time, – let go!

Laurence Hope, from *"The Teak Forest"*

Nobody's perfect.

English proverb

Chapter 5

YOUTH AND AGE

Youth is a blunder; Manhood a struggle; Old Age a regret.

Benjamin Disraeli, *Coningsby*

A man's only as old as the woman he feels.

Groucho Marx

Experience goes to show that age has nothing to do with wisdom.

Begin, baby boy, to recognise your mother with a smile.

Virgil, *Eclogue*

I have no name
I am but two days old.
What shall I call thee?
I happy am.
Joy is my name.
Sweet joy befall thee.

William Blake, from *"Infant Joy"*

"Who was your mother?" "Never had none!" said the child, with another grin. "Never had any mother? What do you mean? Where were you born?" "Never was born!" persisted Topsy: "never had no father, nor mother, nor nothin'. I was raised by a speculator."

Harriet Beecher Stowe, *Uncle Tom's Cabin*

The world has no such flowers in any land,
And no such pearl in any gulf the sea,
As any babe on any mother's knee.

Algernon Charles Swinburne, from *"Pelagius"*

There are times when parenthood seems nothing but
feeding the mouth that bites you.

Peter De Vries, *The Tunnel of Love*

Speak roughly to your little boy,
And beat him when he sneezes;
He only does it to annoy,
Because he knows it teases.

Lewis Carroll, *Alice in Wonderland*

A child enters your home and makes so much noise for twenty years you can hardly stand it – then departs, leaving the house so silent you think you will go mad.

Dr J.A. Holmes, *Dynamic Maturity*

A child deserves the maximum respect; if you ever have something disgraceful in mind, don't ignore your son's tender years.

Juvenal, *Satires*

To make your children *capable of honesty* is the beginning of education.

John Ruskin, *Time and Tide*

A child should always say what's true
And speak when he is spoken to,
And behave mannerly at table;
At least as far as he is able.

Robert Louis Stevenson, from
"Whole Duty of Children"

Teach your child to hold his tongue; he'll learn fast
enough to speak.

Benjamin Franklin, *Poor Richard's Almanac*

Speak when you're spoken to
Do as you're bid.
Shut the door after you,
That's a good kid.

Anon

Anybody who hates children and dogs can't be all bad.

W.C. Fields

When all the world is young, lad,
And all the trees are green;
And every goose a swan, lad,
And every lass a queen;
Then hey for boot and horse, lad,
And round the world away:
Young blood must have its course, lad,
And every dog his day.

Charles Kingsley, *The Water Babies*

When I was a boy of fourteen my father was so ignorant I could hardly stand to have him around. But when I got to be twenty-one, I was astonished at how much he had learned in seven years.

Mark Twain

Grown-ups never understand anything for themselves and it is tiresome for children always and forever explaining things to them.

Antoine de Saint-Exupéry, *The Little Prince*

The joys of parents are secret, and so are their griefs and fears.

Francis Bacon, *Essays*

Nobody can misunderstand a boy like his own mother.

Norman Douglas

An author who speaks about his own books is almost as bad as a mother who talks about her own children.
　　　　Benjamin Disraeli, in Meynell's *Disraeli*

Fathers should neither be seen nor heard. That is the only proper basis for family life.
　　　　Oscar Wilde, *An Ideal Husband*

Children are the anchors that hold a mother to life.
　　　　Sophocles, *Phaedra*

Young women especially have something invested in being *nice people,* and it's only when you have children that you realise you're not a nice person at all, but generally a selfish bully.
　　Fay Weldon, *Independent on Sunday,* 5 May 1991

A man who has been the indisputable favourite of his mother keeps for life the feeling of a conqueror, that confidence of success that often induces real success.

Sigmund Freud, *The Letters of Sigmund Freud*

A mother should give her children a superabundance of enthusiasm, so that after they have lost all they are sure to lose on mixing with the world, enough may still remain to prompt and support them through great actions.

Julius Charles Hare, *Guesses at Truth*

The tree is known by his fruit.

Bible, St Matthew

Ask the mother if the child be like his father.

T. Fuller, *Gnomologia: Adages and Proverbs*

When I was a little boy, I had but little wit,
'Tis a long time ago, and I have no more yet;
Nor ever shall, until that I die,
For the longer I live, the more fool am I.

Nursery rhyme

To be a successful father there's one absolute rule: when you have a kid, don't look at it for the first two years.

Ernest Hemingway, in A.E. Hotchner's
Papa Hemingway

What a comical and affecting memory is that of the first drawing-room in which, at eighteen, one makes one's first appearance alone and without a friend! A glance from a woman was enough to terrify me; the more I wished to please, the more awkward I became. I had the most mistaken ideas about everything. I saw an enemy in every man who looked at me without smiling. But then, in the midst of this fearful unhappiness my shyness caused me, how really beautiful was a beautiful day!

Immanuel Kant

Like other young ladies she is considerably genteeler than her parents.

Jane Austen, letter to her sister Cassandra, 14 Sept. 1804

I have found the best way to give advice to your children is to find out what they want and then advise them to do it.

Harry S. Truman, television interview, 1955

Ye who listen with credulity to the whispers of fancy, and pursue with eagerness the phantoms of hope, who expect that age will perform the promises of youth, and that the deficiencies of the present day will be supplied by the morrow, attend to the history of Rasselas, Prince of Abyssinia.

Dr Johnson, *Rasselas*

Let us then rejoice
While we are young
After the pleasures of youth
And the tiresomeness of old age
Earth will hold us.

Anon

If this was adulthood, the only improvement she could detect in her situation was that now she could eat dessert without eating her vegetables.

Lisa Alther, *Kinflicks*

Youth and discretion are with respect to each other as two parallel lines, which, though infinitely produced, remain still equidistant, and will never coincide.

Tobias Smollett, *Peregrine Pickle*

If youth is the season of hope, it is often so only in the sense that our elders are hopeful about us; for no age is so apt as youth to think its emotions, partings, and resolves are the last of their kind. Each crisis seems final, simply because it is new.

George Eliot, *Middlemarch*

The church bells called across the plain
"Come, people, to your prayers again"
The sun above the stable crept
And bird began to call to bird,
Within the house the servants stirred:
My father and my mother slept.
O happy sleep! O happy love!
I see you as the years go by
United still in constancy,
Warm hearted each to each and proof
Against the world's malicious eye.
Within that household calm and sage
I crawled and stumbled, walked and ran
Up the long steps that lead to man
Until at last I reached the age
Of indiscretion and began
My own unaided pilgrimage.

Ronald McNair Scott, "*Envoi*"

I was twenty-five and too old to be unusual.

James D. Watson, *The Double Helix*

My heart leaps up when I behold
A rainbow in the sky:
So was it when my life began
So is it now I am a man;
So be it when I shall grow old,
Or let me die!
The Child is father of the Man;
And I could wish my days to be
Bound each to each by natural piety.

William Wordsworth, "My Heart Leaps Up"

No young people's evenings are merry, when those they look up to are at home.

Jane Austen, Mansfield Park

All women become like their mothers. That is their tragedy. No man does. That's his.

Oscar Wilde, The Importance of Being Earnest

The youth of the present day are quite monstrous.
They have absolutely no respect for dyed hair.

Oscar Wilde, *Lady Windermere's Fan*

Your children are not your children.
They are the sons and daughters of life's longing for
itself . . .

Kahlil Gibran, from *"The Prophet"*

The daughter begins to bloom before the mother can
be content to fade, and neither can forbear to wish
for the absence of the other.

Dr Johnson, *Rasselas*

Children begin by loving their parents; after a time
they judge them; rarely if ever, do they forgive them.

Oscar Wilde, *A Woman of No Importance*

Despise not thy mother when she is old.

Bible, Proverbs

There is nothing like youth. The middle-aged are mortgaged to Life. The old are in Life's lumber-room. But youth is the Lord of Life. Youth has a kingdom waiting for it.

Oscar Wilde

He who the gods favour dies young.

Plautus, *Bacchides*

Old and young we are all on our last cruise.

Robert Louis Stevenson, *Crabbed Age and Youth*

Crabbed Age and Youth
Cannot live together:
Youth is full of pleasance,
Age is full of care;
Youth like summer morn,
Age like winter weather;
Youth like summer brave,
Age like winter bare.
Youth is full of sport,
Age's breath is short;
Youth is nimble, Age is lame;
Youth is hot and bold,
Age is weak and cold;
Youth is wild, and Age is tame.
Age, I do abhor thee:
Youth I do adore thee . . .

   William Shakespeare, from *"The Passionate Pilgrim"*

Thirty-five is a very attractive age. London is full of women of the very highest birth who have, of their own free choice, remained thirty-five for years.

Oscar Wilde, *The Importance of Being Earnest*

Life Begins at Forty.

Jack Yellen, song title

Forty is a dangerous age, Cynthia.

James Thurber

Forty is the old age of youth; fifty is the youth of old age.

Victor Hugo

She took to telling the truth; she said she was forty-two and five months. It may have been pleasing to the angels, but her elder sister was not gratified.

Saki (H.H. Munro), *Reginald on Besetting Sins*

As long as a woman can look ten years younger than her own daughter, she is perfectly satisfied.

Oscar Wilde, *The Picture of Dorian Gray*

She may very well pass for forty-three
In the dusk with a light behind her!

W.S. Gilbert, *Trial by Jury*

At fifty you have the choice of keeping your figure or your face, and it's *much* better to keep your face.

Dame Barbara Cartland, *Daily Mail*, 10 July 1981

To win back my youth . . . there is nothing I wouldn't
do — except take exercise, get up early, or be a useful
member of the community.

Oscar Wilde, *A Woman of No Importance*

I'm getting deep lines on my forehead;
My face is becoming quite florid.
I measure with dread
My middle-aged spread;
I think growing old is quite horrid.

Ron Rubin

A man shouldn't fool with booze until he's fifty; then
he's a damn fool if he doesn't.

William Faulkner, in James M. Webb and A. Wigfall
Green's *William Faulkner of Oxford*

Whenever a man's friends begin to compliment him about looking young, he may be sure that they think he is growing old.

Washington Irving, *Bracebridge Hall*

Middle age is when, whenever you go on holiday, you pack a sweater.

Denis Norden, *My Word,* BBC Radio, 1976

In youth we tend to look forward; in old age we tend to look back; in middle age we tend to look worried.

Anon

A lady of a certain age, which means
Certainly aged.

Byron, from *"Don Juan"*

Now that I'm sixty, I see why the idea of elder wisdom has passed from currency.

> John Updike, *New Yorker,* Nov. 1992

Wrinkles should merely indicate where smiles have been.

> Mark Twain, *Following the Equator*

What is the price of Experience? Do men buy it for a
    song?
Or wisdom for a dance in the street? No, it is bought
    with the price
Of all that a man hath, his house, his wife, his
    children...

> William Blake, *Vala or The Four Zoas*

Experience teacheth Fools; and he is a great one, that will not learn by it.

Thomas Fuller, *Gnomologia no. 1484*

One starts to get young at the age of sixty and then it is too late.

Pablo Picasso, *Sunday Times,* 20 Oct. 1963

Seventy is old enough. After that there is too much risk.

Mark Twain, *Following the Equator*

Not knowing at thirty what I knew about women at sixty.

Arthur Miller, *on being asked if he had any regrets on his seventieth birthday*

The years teach much which the days never know.

> R.W. Emerson, *Essays*

~{●}~

If youth knew, if age could.

> Henri Estienne, *Les Prémices*

~{●}~

Considering the alternative . . . it's not too bad at all.

> Maurice Chevalier on old age

~{●}~

One of the many pleasures of old age is giving things up.

> Malcolm Muggeridge

Good temper is one of the great preservers of the features.

James Northcote, recorded by William Hazlitt

Anyone can get old. All you have to do is to live long enough.

Groucho Marx

See how the world its veterans rewards!
A youth of frolics, and old age of cards.

Alexander Pope, *Moral Essays*

The greatest problem about old age is the fear that it may go on too long.

A.J.P. Taylor, *Observer*, 1981

Whatever a man's age may be, he can reduce it by several years by putting a bright-coloured flower in his buttonhole.

Mark Twain

Youth has no age.

Pablo Picasso, in Dore Ahston's *Picasso on Art*

When you are younger you get blamed for crimes you never committed and when you're older you begin to get credit for virtues you never possessed. It evens itself out.

I.F. Stone, *International Herald Tribune*,
16 March 1988

I think they deserve to have more than twelve years between the ages of 28 and 40.

> James Thurber, on women and age, in *Time*,
> 15 Aug. 1960

We need the enthusiasm of the young. We need their *joie de vivre*. In it is reflected something of the original joy God had in creating man.

> Pope John Paul II, *Crossing the Threshold of Hope*

I don't feel eighty. In fact I don't feel anything until noon, then it's time for my nap.

> Bob Hope, *International Herald Tribune*, 3 Aug. 1990

Life is one long process of getting tired.

Samuel Butler, *Notebooks*

Alas, it is not the child but the boy that generally survives in a man.

Arthur Helps

Growing old is like being increasingly penalized for a crime you haven't committed.

Anthony Powell, *Temporary Kings*

We live and learn, but not the wiser grow.

John Pomfret, *Reason*

"You are old," said the youth, "one would hardly
      suppose
That your eye was as steady as ever;
Yet you balanced an eel on the end of your nose –
What made you so awfully clever?"

"I have answered three questions, and that is enough,"
Said his father. "Don't give yourself airs!
Do you think I can listen all day to such stuff?
Be off, or I'll kick you downstairs!"
      Lewis Carroll, from *"You Are Old Father William"*

It doth not become green heads to advise grey hairs.
      Henry Fielding, *Joseph Andrews*

You know you're getting old when the candles cost
more than the cake.

      Bob Hope

The old believe everything: the middle-aged suspect everything: the young know everything.

Oscar Wilde, *Phrases and Philosophies for the Use of the Young*

We're like bad architecture or an old whore. If you stick around long enough, you eventually get respectable.

Jerry Garcia on the rock group Grateful Dead, in S. Troy's *Captain Trips*

How true it is, yet how inconsistent, that while all desire to live long, we have all a horror of being old.

Fanny Burney, *Cecilia*

Tho' much is taken, much abides; and tho'
We are not now that strength which in old days
Moved earth and heaven; that which we are, we are;
One equal temper of heroic hearts,
Made weak by time and fate, but strong in will
To strive, to seek, to find, and not to yield.

Alfred, Lord Tennyson, from *"Ulysses"*

Autumn is mellower, and what we lose in flowers, we
more than gain in fruits.

Samuel Butler, *The Way of All Flesh*

Thoughtfulness begets wrinkles.

Charles Dickens, *Barnaby Rudge*

The body of Benjamin Franklin, printer
(like the cover of an old book,
its contents worn out,
and stript of its lettering and gilding)
lies here, food for worms.
Yet the work itself shall not be lost,
for it will, as he believed, appear once more
in a new
and more beautiful edition,
corrected and amended
by its Author.

> Benjamin Franklin, epitaph for himself

We are things of a day. What are we? What are we
   not?
The shadow of a dream
is man, no more.

> Pindar, *Odes*

Experience is of no ethical value. It is merely the name men give to their mistakes.

Oscar Wilde, *The Picture of Dorian Gray*

As a white candle
In a holy place,
So is the beauty
Of an aged face.

Joseph Campbell, *The Old Woman*

Chapter 6

TIME FLIES

Snatching the eternal out of the desperately
fleeting is the great magic trick of human
existence.
      Tennessee Williams, in *New York Times*

My people need time, if only to look at a tree.
To sit down each day on the threshold in front
of the same tree with the same branches. And
little by little the tree reveals itself to them.
      Antoine de Saint-Exupéry, *The Little Prince*

Some timely thoughts . . .

Time wounds all heels.
Groucho Marx, *Marx Brothers Go West* (film)

A French five minutes is ten minutes shorter than a Spanish five minutes, but slightly longer than an English five minutes which is usually ten minutes.
Guy Bellamy, *Comedy Hotel*

Time travels in divers paces with divers persons. I'll tell you who Time ambles withal, who Time trots withal, who Time gallops withal and who he stands still withal.
William Shakespeare, *As You Like It*

Three o'clock is always too late or too early for anything you want to do.
Jean-Paul Sartre, *La Nausée*

A man who has to be punctually at a certain place at five o'clock has the whole afternoon ruined for him already.

Lin Yutang, *The Importance of Living*

When as a child I laughed and wept,
Time crept,
When as a youth I dreamed and talked,
Time walked,
When I became a full-grown man,
Time ran,
And later as I older grew
Time flew.
Soon shall I find when travelling on
Time gone.
Will Christ have saved my soul by then?
Amen.

Verses inscribed on the pendulum of the clock in
St Lawrence's church, Bidborough, Kent

Worlds on worlds are rolling ever
From creation to decay,
Like the bubbles on a river
Sparkling, bursting, borne away.

Percy Bysshe Shelley, from *"Hellas"*

If I say to the moment: "Stay now! You are so
beautiful!"

Johann Wolfgang von Goethe, *Faust*

The Moving Finger writes; and having writ
Moves on: nor all thy Piety or Wit
Shall lure it back to cancel half a Line,
Nor all thy tears wash out a Word of it.

Edward Fitzgerald (translator), from
"The Rubáiyát of Omar Khayyám"

Nothing puzzles me more than time and space; and yet nothing troubles me less, as I never think about them.

Charles Lamb, letter to T. Manning, 2 Jan. 1810

The universe is not hostile, nor yet is it friendly. It is simply indifferent.

John Haynes Holmes, *Sensible Man's View of Religion*

To choose time is to save time.

Frances Bacon, *Essays*

Remember that time is money.

Benjamin Franklin, *Advice to a Young Tradesman*

Fear no more the heat o' the sun,
Nor the furious winter's rages;
Thou thy worldly task hast done,
Home art gone, and ta'en thy wages:
Golden lads and girls all must,
As chimney-sweepers, come to dust.

> William Shakespeare, *Cymbeline*

The glories of our blood and state
Are shadows, not substantial things;
There is no armour against Fate;
Death lays his icy hand on kings.
Sceptre and Crown
Must tumble down,
And in the dust be equal made
With the poor crooked scythe and spade.

> James Shirley, *The Glories of our Blood and State*

There is nothing stable in the world – uproar's your only music.

John Keats, letter to George and Thomas Keats, 13 Jan. 1819

~❦~

No arts; no letters; no society; and which is worst of all, continual fear and danger of violent death; and the life of man, solitary, poor, nasty, brutish and short.

Thomas Hobbes, *Leviathan*

~❦~

Time and tide and newspapers wait for no man.

C. Aird, *Eloquent X*

~❦~

The less one has to do the less time one finds to do it in.

Lord Chesterfield, *Letters*

Nothing is worth more than this day.
>Johann Wolfgang von Goethe, *Maxims
>and Reflections*

Art is long, and Time is fleeting,
And our hearts, though stout and brave,
Still, like muffled drums, are beating
Funeral marches to the grave.
>Henry Wadsworth Longfellow,
>from *"A Psalm of Life"*

The bloom is gone, and with the bloom go I.
>Matthew Arnold, from *"Thyrsis"*

She dwells with Beauty – Beauty that must die;
And Joy, whose hand is ever at his lips
Bidding adieu . . .
>John Keats, from *"Ode on Melancholy"*

Had we been born of a fallen angel, then the contemporary predicament would lie as far beyond solution as it would lie beyond explanation . . . The miracle of man is not how far he has sunk but how magnificently he has risen.

Robert Ardrey, *African Genesis*

Come what may,
Time and the hour runs through the roughest day.

William Shakespeare, *Macbeth*

All shall be well, and all shall be well, and all manner of thing shall be well.

Julian of Norwich, *Revelations of Divine Love*

Time is the great physician.

Benjamin Disraeli, *Endymion*

Cease, mortals, to conserve your prime
In vain attempts at killing time
For Time, alas, what e'er you do
Is sure to end in killing you.

Lord Palmerston

History is not what happened, it is what you can remember.

W.C. Sellar and R.J. Yateman, 1066 and All That

The poetry of history lies in the quasi-miraculous fact that once, on this earth, once, on this familiar spot of ground, walked other men and women, as actual as we are today, thinking their own thoughts, swayed by their own passions, but now all gone, one generation vanishing after another, gone as utterly as we ourselves shall shortly be gone like a ghost at cockcrow.

G.M. Trevelyan, Autobiography of an Historian

No great man lives in vain. The history of the world is but the biography of great men.

Thomas Carlyle, *On Heroes, Hero-Worship, and the Heroic*

History is bunk.

Henry Ford

Ambition is a meteor-gleam;
Fame a restless airy dream;
Pleasures, insects on the wing
Round peace, th' tend'rest flow'r of spring . . .

Robert Burns, from "*Written in Friars Carse Hermitage*"

When your watch gets out of order you have the choice of two things to do: throw it in the fire or take it to the watch-tinker. The former is quicker.

Mark Twain, *Following the Equator*

Letting go all else, cling to the following few truths. Remember that man lives only in the present, in this fleeting instant: all the rest of life is either past and gone, or not yet revealed. This mortal life is a little thing, lived in a little corner of the earth; and little, too, is the longest fame to come – dependent as it is on a succession of fast-perishing little men who have no knowledge even of their own selves, much less of one long dead and gone.

Marcus Aurelius, *Meditations*

Boast not thyself of tomorrow; for thou knowest not what a day may bring forth.

Bible, Proverbs

The best fruits are those which fall by themselves when they are ripe.

Ricciotti

But the fruit that can fall without shaking
Indeed is too mellow for me.
    Lady Mary Worthley Montagu, *Letters and Works*

Time is like a fashionable host
That slightly shakes his parting guest by the hand,
And with his arms outstretch'd, as he would fly,
Grasps in the comer; welcome ever smiles,
And farewell goes out sighing.
    William Shakespeare, *Troilus and Cressida*

Time is the only critic without ambition.
    John Steinbeck, in *Writers at Work*,
    ed. George Plimpton

Our lives are dominated by symbols of our own making. Once we had invented time . . . we became in thrall to the notion . . .

Gore Vidal, *Observer*, 27 Aug. 1989

The cradle rocks above an abyss . . .

Vladimir Nabokov, *Speak, Memory*

Today lays many plans for years to come.

English proverb

Patience is sweet.

Bedouin saying

There is a time for every matter under heaven
a time to be born, and a time to die;
a time to plant, and a time to pluck up what is
planted;
a time to kill, and a time to heal . . .
Bible, Ecclesiastes

Procrastination is the thief of time.
Edward Young, *The Complaint: Night Thoughts*

Punctuality is the thief of time.
Oscar Wilde, *The Picture of Dorian Gray*

Punctuality is the virtue of the bored.
Evelyn Waugh, *Diaries of Evelyn Waugh,*
ed. Michael Davies

Tomorrow is another day.

English proverb

～•～

Even such is Time, which takes in trust
Our youth, our joys, and all we have,
And pays us but with age and dust;
Who in the dark and silent grave,
When we have wandered all our ways,
Shuts up the story of our days:
And from which earth, and grave, and dust,
The Lord shall raise me up, I trust.

Sir Walter Ralegh, lines found in his Bible
after his death

～•～

One thing at a time is my motto – and just play that thing for all its worth, even if it's only two pair and a jack.

Mark Twain, *Connecticut Yankee*

No time like the present.

"Such," said he, "O King, seems to me the present life of men on earth, in comparison with that time which is to us uncertain, as if when on a winter's night you sit feasting with your ealdormans and thanes – a single sparrow should fly swiftly into the hall, and coming in at one door, instantly fly out through another. In that time in which it is indoors it is indeed not touched by the fury of the winter, but yet this smallest space of calmness being passed almost in a flash, from winter going into winter again, it is lost to your eyes. Somewhat like this appears the life of man; but of what follows or what went before we are utterly ignorant."

The Venerable Bede, *Ecclesiastical History*

Nothing is worth more than this day.
Johann Wolfgang von Goethe, *Maxims and Reflections*

The soul's dark cottage, battered and decayed,
Lets in new light through chinks that Time has made;
Stronger, by weakness, wiser men become,
As they draw nearer to their eternal home.

Edmund Waller, from *"Of the Last Verses in a Book"*

We take no note of Time
But from its Loss.

Edward Young, *The Complaint: Night Thoughts*

Things ain't what they used to be and probably never
was.

Will Rogers

Nostalgia isn't what it used to be.

Anon

The past is a foreign country; they do things differently there.

L.P. Hartley, *The Go-Between*

I bind unto myself this day
The virtues of the starlit heaven,
The glorious sun's life giving ray,
The whiteness of the moon at even,
The flashing of the lightning free,
The whirling wind's tempestuous shocks,
The stable earth, the deep salt sea
Around the old, eternal rocks.

St Patrick, from *"The Breastplate,"*
tr. Cecil Frances Alexander from the Ancient Irish

Morning is wiser than evening.

Russian proverb

The present moment is a powerful goddess.

Johann Wolfgang von Goethe, *Tasso*

Nothing in the voice of the cicada
Intimates
How soon it will die.

Matsuō Bash, *"Nothing in the Voice of the Cicada"*

Fair daffodils, we weep to see
You haste away so soon:
As yet the early-rising sun
Has not attained his noon.

Robert Herrick, from *"To Daffodils"*

Carpe diem, quam minimum credula postero.
(Seize the day, and put as little trust as you can in the morrow.)

Horace, *Odes*

Take therefore no thought for the morrow: for the morrow shall take thought for the things of itself. Sufficient unto the day is the evil thereof.

Bible, St Matthew

I think time is a merciless thing. I think life is a process of burning oneself out and time is the fire that burns you. But I think the spirit of man is a good adversary.

Tennessee Williams, *New York Post*, 13 April 1958

Time like an ever-rolling stream
Bears all its sons away;
They fly forgotten as a dream
Dies at the opening day.

Isaac Watts, *Psalms*

❧❦❧

Live not as though there were a thousand years ahead
of you. Fate is at your elbow, make yourself good
while life and power are still yours.

Marcus Aurelius, *Meditations*

❧❦❧

Vanity of vanities, saith the Preacher, vanity of
vanities; all is vanity.

What profit hath a man of all his labour which he
taketh under the sun?

One generation passeth away, and another
generation cometh.

Bible, Ecclesiastes

If the past cannot teach the present and the father cannot teach the son, then history need not have bothered to go on, and the world has wasted a great deal of time.

> Russell Hoban, *The Lion of Boaz-Jachin and Jachin-Boaz*

The truth is that our race survived ignorance; it is our scientific genius that will do us in.

> Stephen Vizinczey, *Truth and Lies in Literature*

The end of the human race will be that it will eventually die of civilization.

> R.W. Emerson

Let the world slide, let the world go;
A fig for care, and a fig for woe!
If I can't pay, why I can owe,
And death makes equal the high and low.
John Heywood, *"Be Merry, Friends"*

It was the best of times, it was the worst of times, it was the age of wisdom, it was the age of foolishness, it was the epoch of belief, it was the epoch of incredulity, it was the season of Light, it was the season of Darkness, it was the spring of hope, it was the winter of despair, we had everything before us, we had nothing before us, we were all going direct to Heaven, we were all going direct the other way.
The opening sentence of Charles Dickens'
A Tale of Two Cities

Oh, come with old Khayyám, and leave the Wise
To talk: one thing is certain, that Life flies;
One thing is certain, and the Rest is Lies;
The Flower that once hath blown for ever dies.
Edward Fitzgerald (translator), from
"The Rubáiyát of Omar Khayyám"

Time flies over us, but leaves its shadow behind.
Nathaniel Hawthorne, *The Marble Faun*

Time is the only thing that can't be spared.
Charles Dickens, *Bleak House*

Time ruthlessly destroys his own romances.
Thomas Hardy, *Tess of the D'Urbervilles*

Time is a great teacher, but unfortunately it kills all its pupils.

Berlioz, *Themes and Variations*

Dost thou love life, then do not squander time, for that's the stuff life is made of.

Benjamin Franklin, *The Way to Wealth*

Eternity's a terrible thought. I mean, where's it all going to end?

Tom Stoppard, *Rosencrantz and Guildenstern Are Dead*

It is later than you think.

From a sundial

Chapter 7

FINAL REFLECTIONS

The owl of Minerva spreads its wings only with the falling of the dusk.

G.W.F. Hegel, *Philosophy of Right*
tr. T.M. Knox

Where shall wisdom be found, and where is the place of understanding?

Bible, Job

For those seeking truth, some philosophy to end with.

I am certain of nothing but the holiness of the heart's affections, and the truth of imagination – what the imagination seizes as beauty must be truth – whether it existed before or not.

John Keats, letter to Benjamin Bailey,
22 Nov. 1817

Then the Stork
Gave a philosophic talk
Till the Hippopotomi
Said: "Ask no further
What am *I?*"

L. Leslie Brooke, *Johnny Crow's Garden*

The fox knows many things – the hedgehog one *big* one.

Archilochus, in *Anthologia Lyrica Graeca*,
ed. E. Diehl

Pure and complete sorrow is as impossible as pure and complete joy.

Leo Tolstoy, *War and Peace*

They also serve who only stand and wait.

John Milton, *On His Blindness*

Where ignorance is bliss, 'tis folly to be wise.

English proverb

Ful wys is he that can him-selven knowe.

Geoffrey Chaucer, *Canterbury Tales*

One is one's own refuge, who else could be the refuge?

> The Buddha, *Dhammapada*, (in Walpola Rahula's
> *What the Buddha Taught*)

He knows the universe and does not know himself.

> Jean de la Fontaine, *Fables*

Two men look through the same bars:
One sees the mud, and one the stars.

> Frederick Langbridge, *A Cluster of Quiet Thoughts*

The wise through excess of wisdom is made a fool.

> R.W. Emerson, *Essays*

I gave my heart to know wisdom, and to know madness and folly; I perceived that this also is vexation of spirit. For in much wisdom is much grief.

Bible, Ecclesiastes

Here are my three treasures. Guard and keep them! The first is pity; the second, frugality; the third, refusal to be "foremost of all things under heaven."

Tao Te Ching

Losing faith in your own singularity is the start of wisdom, I suppose . . .

Peter Conrad, *Down Under: Revisiting Tasmania*

Conquer anger by love, evil by good; conquer the miser with liberality, and the liar with truth.

The Buddha, *Dhammapada* (in Walpola Rahula's *What the Buddha Taught*)

Hope springs eternal in the human breast:
Man never Is, but always To be blest.

Alexander Pope, from *"An Essay on Man"*

Nothing worth knowing can be understood with the mind.

Woody Allen, *Manhattan* (film)

The heart has its reasons which reason knows nothing of.

Blaise Pascal, *Pensées*

Golf is a good walk spoiled.

Mark Twain

An acre in Middlesex is better than a principality in Utopia.

> Thomas Babington Macaulay, *Francis Bacon*

There once was a man who said "God
Must think it exceedingly odd
If he finds that this tree
Continues to be
When there's no one about in the Quad."

> Ronald Knox (attrib.) *"Idealism"*

Dear Sir, Your astonishment's odd:
I am always about in the Quad.
And that's why the tree
Will continue to be,
Since observed by Yours faithfully, God.

> Anon, reply to *"Idealism"*

Nothing ever becomes real until it is experienced –
even a proverb is no proverb to you till your life has
illustrated it.

John Keats, letter to George and Georgiana Keats,
May 1819

When all is done, human life is, at the greatest and
the best, but like a froward child, that must be play'd
with and humoured a little to keep it quiet till it falls
asleep, and then the care is over.

Sir William Temple, *Essay on Poetry*

Great joys, like griefs, are silent.

Shackerley Marmion, *Holland's Leaguer*

There is no greater anguish,
Than to remember in black hours of sorrows,
The joyful times . . .

> Dante, *Inferno*

When Time, who steals our years away
Shall steal our pleasures too
The memory of the past will stay
And half our joys renew.

> Thomas Moore

He who has his hand in the water is not like him who
has his hand in the fire.
(Attitudes are formed by circumstances.)
   Arab proverb in Primrose Arnander and Ashkhain
      Skipwith's *The Son of a Duck is a Floater*

Ask yourself whether you are happy, and you cease to be so.

John Stuart Mill, *Autobiography*

Great is Truth, and mighty above all things.

Apocrypha, *I Esdras*

Even if all his life a fool associates with a wise man, he will not understand the Truth, even as the spoon [does not understand] the flavour of the soup.

The Buddha, *Dhammapada* (in Walpola Rahula's *What the Buddha Taught*)

There are no such things as facts, only interpretation.
Friedrich Nietzsche, in *Modernism*,
eds Malcolm Bradbury and James McFarlane

～｛●｝～

In this world nothing can be said to be certain, except death and taxes.
Benjamin Franklin, letter to Jean Baptiste Le Roy,
13 Nov. 1789

～｛●｝～

"It was as true," said Mr Barkis . . . "as taxes is. And nothing's truer than them."
Charles Dickens, *David Copperfield*

～｛●｝～

We are never as fortunate or as unfortunate as we suppose.
Duc de la Rochefoucauld, *Maxims*

In troubled water you can scarce see your face, or see it very little, till the water be quiet and stand still. So in troubled times you can see little Truth; when times are quiet and settled, Truth appears.

John Selden

Blessed is he who expects nothing, for he shall never be disappointed.

Alexander Pope, letter to John Gay

If you do not expect the unexpected, you will never find it.

Heraclitus

Cast thy bread upon the waters: for thou shalt find it after many days.

Bible, Ecclesiastes

If there be righteousness in our hearts,
There will be beauty in our characters.
If there be beauty in our characters,
There will be harmony in our homes.
If there be harmony in our homes,
There will be order in the nations.
If there be order in the nations,
There will be peace in the world.

Confucius

Nature's greatest masterpiece, an elephant,
The only harmless great thing.

John Donne, *The Progress of the Soul*

To make judgements about great and high things, a
soul of the same stature is needed; otherwise we
ascribe to them that vice which is our own.

Montaigne, *Essays*

There are many wonderful things, and nothing is more wonderful than man.

Sophocles, *Antigone*

Humour is mankind's greatest blessing.

Mark Twain, *Biography*

This world is a comedy to those that think, a tragedy to those that feel.

Horace Walpole, 4th Earl of Orford, letter to Anne, Countess of Upper Ossory, 16 Aug. 1776

The optimist proclaims that we live in the best of all possible worlds; and the pessimist fears this is true.

James Branch Cabell, *The Silver Stallion*

A little flesh, a little breath, and a Reason to rule all —
that is myself.

Marcus Aurelius, *Meditations*

~·❧·~

If only God would give me some clear sign! Like
making a large deposit in my name at a Swiss bank.

Woody Allen, *New Yorker,* 5 Nov. 1973

~·❧·~

A little learning is a dangerous thing;
Drink deep, or taste not the Pieran spring:
There shallow draughts intoxicate the brain,
And drinking largely sobers us again.

Alexander Pope, from *"An Essay on Criticism"*

~·❧·~

The mind is its own place, and in it self
Can make a Heaven of Hell, a Hell of Heaven.

John Milton, from *"Paradise Lost"*

There is nothing either good or bad, but thinking makes it so.

William Shakespeare, *Hamlet*

~ ❦ ~

Life doesn't imitate art, it imitates bad television.

Woody Allen, *Husbands and Wives* (film)

~ ❦ ~

Oysters are more beautiful than any religion. There's nothing in Christianity or Buddhism that quite matches the sympathetic unselfishness of an oyster.

Saki (H.H. Munro), *The Chronicles of Clovis*

~ ❦ ~

A thing of beauty is a joy for ever:
Its loveliness increases; it will never
Pass into nothingness, but still will keep
A bower quiet for us, and a sleep
Full of sweet dreams, and health and quiet breathing.

John Keats, from *"Endymion"*

Music is an echo of the innumerable voices of Eternity.

Sir Thomas Beecham

~•~

God makes man lose his donkey so that he can give him the pleasure of finding it again.

Turkish proverb

~•~

Habit is a gift from God to make up for the loss of happiness.

Alexander Pushkin, *Eugène Onegin*

~•~

We are here and it is now. Further than that, all human knowledge is moon-shine.

H.L. Mencken

There are more things in heaven and earth, Horatio,
Than are dreamt of in your philosophy.

William Shakespeare, *Hamlet*

My idea of heaven is, eating *pâté de foie gras* to the
sound of trumpets.

Sydney Smith, in Hesketh Pearson's
The Smith of Smiths

May the road rise to meet you
May the wind be always at your back
The sun shine warm upon your face
The rain fall soft upon your fields
And until we meet again
May God hold you in the hollow
Of His Hand.

Irish blessing

Laughter is the sun that drives the winter from the human face.

Victor Hugo

~ ❦ ~

There is nothing in the world constant, but inconstancy.

Jonathan Swift, *On the Faculties of the Mind*

~ ❦ ~

Nowhere probably is there more true feeling, and nowhere worse taste, than in a churchyard.

Benjamin Jowett, in *Letters of Benjamin Jowett*, eds Evelyn Abbott and Lewis Campbell

~ ❦ ~

Soap and education are not as sudden as a massacre, but they are more deadly in the long run.

Mark Twain, *Sketches New & Old*

Conceit may puff a man up, but never prop him up.

John Ruskin, *True and Beautiful: Morals and Religion*

A fear of becoming ridiculous is the best guide in life.

Benjamin Disraeli

You cannot learn to skate without being ridiculous ...The ice of life is slippery.

Bernard Shaw, *Fanny's First Play*

...be an enthusiast in the front part of your heart and ironical in the back.

Oliver Wendell Holmes, Jr

One swallow doesn't make a summer but too many swallows make a fall.

George D. Prentice

There's something about a closet that makes a skeleton terribly restless.

John Barrymore

He who neglects to drink of the spring of experience is apt to die of thirst in the desert of ignorance.

Ling Po, *Epigram*

If no Pain were, how judge we of Pleasure?
If no Work, where's the solace of Leisure?
What's White, if no Black?
What's Wealth, if no Lack?
If no Loss, how our Gain could we measure?

William Bliss

The facts of a person's life will, like murder, come out.

Norman Sherry, *International Herald Tribune,*
15 Sept. 1989

If a man begin with certainties, he shall end in doubts; but if he will begin with doubts, he shall end in certainties.

Francis Bacon, *The Advancement of Learning*

There is no good in arguing with the inevitable. The only argument available with an east wind is to put on your overcoat.

James Russell Lowell, *Democracy and Other Addresses*

Have nothing in your houses that you do not know to be useful, or believe to be beautiful.

William Morris, *Hopes and Fears for Art*

❧

The most beautiful things in the world are the most useless – peacocks and lilies for instance.

John Ruskin, *The Stones of Venice*

❧

Mediocrity knows nothing higher than itself, but talent instantly recognises genius.

Arthur Conan Doyle, *The Valley of Fear*

❧

Knowledge is proud that she has learnt so much,
Wisdom is humble that she knows no more.

William Cowper, from *"The Winter Walk at Noon"*

There is one true coin for which all things ought to be exchanged, and that is wisdom.

Plato, *Phaedo*

If there is no money in poetry, neither is there poetry in money.

Robert Graves

To learn to draw a flower it is best to place a blossoming plant in a deep hollow in the ground and to look upon it. Then all its qualities may be grasped. To learn to draw a bamboo, take a branch and cast its shadow upon a white wall on a moonlight night; then its true outline can be obtained. To learn to paint a landscape, too, the method is the same. An artist should identify himself with the landscape and watch it until its significance is revealed to him.

Kuo Hsi

Look at the stars! look, look up at the skies!
O look at all the fire-folk sitting in the air!
The bright boroughs, the circle-citadels there!
    Gerard Manley Hopkins, from *"The Starlight Night"*

There are three ingredients in the good life: learning,
earning and yearning.
    Christopher Morley, *Parnassus on Wheels*

Prosperity doth best discover vice, but adversity doth
best discover virtue.
    Francis Bacon, *The Elements of Common Law*

There is no duty we so much underrate as the duty of
being happy.
    Robert Louis Stevenson, *Virginibus Puerisque*

Goodness does not more certainly make men happy
than happiness makes them good.
    Walter Savage Landor, *Imaginary Conversations*:
        Lord Brooke and Sir Philip Sidney

I know nothing except the fact of my ignorance.
    Socrates, in Diogenes Laertius,
        Lives of the Philosophers

Oh don't the days seem lank and long
When all goes right and nothing wrong,
And isn't your life extremely flat
With nothing whatever to grumble at!
    W.S. Gilbert and Arthur Sullivan, *Princess Ida*

Science without religion is lame, religion without science is blind.

Albert Einstein, *Out of My Later Years*

~⟨●⟩~

The more opinions you have, the less you see.

Wim Wenders, *Evening Standard*, 25 April 1990

~⟨●⟩~

I have tried too in my time to be a philosopher; but, I don't know how, cheerfulness was always breaking in.

Oliver Edwards, in Boswell's *Life of Johnson*

~⟨●⟩~

Truly there is a tide in the affairs of men; but there is no gulf stream setting forever in one direction.

James Russell Lowell, *Among My Books*

The trouble with our age is that it is all signpost and no destination.

Louis Kronenberger, *Company Manners*

~⚘~

How can you get onto Route 66 when you live off the M1?

Jarvis Cocker on the "American dream," in Susan Wilson's *Pulp: The Tommorrow People*

~⚘~

So many men, so many opinions.

Terence, *Phormio*

~⚘~

People who count their chickens before they are hatched act very wisely: because chickens run about so absurdly afterwards that it is impossible to count them accurately.

Oscar Wilde

We have sought truth, and sometimes perhaps found it. But have we had any *fun?*

Benjamin Jowett

Nothing is so useless as a general maxim.

Thomas Babington Macaulay, *Literary Essays*

Acknowledgements

Every effort has been made to trace copyright holders in all copyright material in this book. The editors regret if there has been an oversight and suggest the publisher be contacted in any such event. The following permissions are gratefully acknowledged:

The Society of Authors as the literary representative of the Estate of Norman Douglas;

The Society of Authors as the literary representative of the Estate of L.P.Hartley;

The Society of Authors as the literary representative of the Estate of Virginia Woolf;

The Society of Authors, on behalf of the Bernard Shaw Estate;

The Society of Authors as the literary representative of the Estate of Compton Mackenzie;

From *Letters from London* by Julian Barnes, and from *Janus, A Summing Up* by Arthur Koestler, reprinted by permission of the Peters Fraser & Dunlop Group Ltd.

From *The Message to the Planet* by Iris Murdoch, reprinted by kind permission of the Estate of Dame Iris Murdoch.

From *"Politics and the English Language"* by George Orwell, reprinted by kind permission of A.M. Heath & Co Ltd.

From *"And Even Now"* by Max Beerbohm, reproduced by permission of London Management.

From *Rosencrantz and Guildenstern Are Dead* by Tom Stoppard, reproduced by kind permission of the author, Faber & Faber Ltd and Grove Press.